A CANDID CRITIQUE
OF
BOOK PUBLISHING

A CANDID CRITIQUE
OF
BOOK PUBLISHING

by Curtis G. Benjamin

R. R. BOWKER COMPANY
New York & London, 1977

Published by R. R. Bowker Company
1180 Avenue of the Americas, New York, N.Y. 10036
Copyright © 1977 by Xerox Corporation
All rights reserved
Printed and bound in the United States of America

Library of Congress Cataloging in Publication Data

Benjamin, Curtis G   1901–
  A candid critique of book publishing.

  Bibliography: p.
  Includes index.
  1. Publishers and publishing. I. Title.
Z278.B42   070.5'73   77-21286
ISBN 0-8352-1033-2

To Martin Foss and Jim Thompson
who taught me the fundamentals

Contents

Preface

This book had an unusual and uncertain genesis.

Several years ago, flying back to New York from the Frankfurt Book Fair, I found myself sitting, accidentally, with a good-buddy fellow publisher. Traveling first class we were; and feeling the fatigue of five days and ten nights (or so it seemed) at the fair, we were lapping up the free drinks like those goofs who gulp down Pepsi on TV. Soon my good-buddy seatmate allowed that we were timely, as well as accidentally, met. He had been thinking for some time, he said, that he would like to publish a collection of my papers on book publishing. Would I be interested?

His question surprised me, for he was the head-of-house of a large commercial firm, not a scrounging editor in a smaller, hungry one. But, feeling expansive under the influence, and being truly flattered by the suggestion, I immediately agreed to listen to a proposal.

He thought that about 20 of my "seminal" papers would be enough for the collection. But he would impose one condition: that I should write a long introduction to the volume—something "autobiographical, anecdotal, and philosophical" in nature. Something like 40 to 50 pages would be about right, he thought. Still I could make it longer or shorter, as I liked. Surely, one good-buddy publisher should never be too exacting on another good-buddy publisher.

Given my weakness for wanting to say something at every opportunity about any aspect of book publishing, I agreed immediately. So we shook hands and had another drink on it—all before our dinner was served. How simply and quickly a deal can be made between two old hands at book publishing!

Later, when I sat down to fill my friend's prescription, I wrote far too much. And I made another mistake: I asked two of my McGraw-Hill associates, Edward Booher and Robert Slaughter, to read draft manuscript as I finished each section. Why, they asked, did I not include more about my experiences at McGraw-Hill as I went along? Then, after the whole piece was finished, many of these added passages could be excised, and thus I should have in them the start of an informal account of my earlier years with the company—something to which they had long wanted me to set my hand. It seemed to be a good idea, for I had been putting off this writing task for several years.

Setting off on the new course, I soon saw that I was trying to write one account of two subjects. Clearly it would not work. And just then came a more serious contretemps: my good-buddy prospective publisher resigned his job and went to another firm, one that publishes neither general nor professional books. So there I was, an experienced publisher in an awkward position as a would-be author, because patently I had to look upon that over-the-Atlantic agreement as no more than a personal commitment.

Still I decided to finish the manuscript, leaving out the McGraw-Hill parts and producing a long essay on book publishing in general, expounded with a *de rigueur* set of topical headings. (Oh, how hard the author has to labor to follow so easily given editorial advice!)

Then when my still-trusted associates read the stripped-down manuscript, they said, "Swell! But you really should turn this overly long essay into a short book." So again I started afresh, mainly because I had meanwhile reviewed some 50-odd of my published papers and had found them to be surprisingly repetitious and to betray an astonishing rate of obsolescence.

Certain sections of the longish essay lent themselves to easy expansion into short chapters; nor was it difficult to rewrite and update several of my "seminal" papers as additional chapters that are relevant to book publishing today. This procedure explains the loosely structured nature of the book and why it cannot be taken as a systematic or comprehensive treatment of its subject. But in the end it did result, I trust, in a volume that will be much more useful and durable than the kind of work that was proposed by my good-buddy companion on that return-from-Frankfurt flight.

Some older readers may recognize that Chapters 10 and 11 are developed from certain ideas that I expressed some years ago in two articles published in the *Saturday Review*—one entitled "The Industry that Disdains Success," the other, "Book Publishing's Hidden Bonanza." Chapters 6 and 7 draw upon a paper written in 1974 for the National Commission on Libraries and Information Science. Chapter 15 draws upon an earlier paper on which my former associate Gordon Graham was collaborator. Chapter 16 is based on a 1972 paper for the First International Comprint Conference at Geneva; it was reprinted in the same year by *The Bookseller* of London. Likewise, Chapter 17 is based upon a paper written for the 1969 Southeast Asia Symposia on Book Development, sponsored by the United States Information Agency in New Delhi and Singapore, and later printed in the *UNESCO Newsletter* of the Regional Center for Book Development in Asia at Karachi.

I must thank the original publishers of all these papers for their permission to use them as source material, and especially the publisher of the *Saturday Review*, where the policy on reprint use by authors has always been generous.

Also, I want to thank my dear friends Edward Booher and the late Robert Slaughter for their interest in the first drafts of the manuscript. And I owe an even larger debt of gratitude to Mr. Booher and to Dan Lacy and Roger Donald for criticizing the later and transmuted revisions. Charles Lieb, Esquire, read the chapter on copyright, and Townsend Hoopes read the chapters on trade associations and government relations. All were very helpful, and especially so in challenging my prejudices and conventional wisdom on certain debatable attitudes and declarations.

Also, I want to thank Chandler Grannis, my "advisory editor" at Bowker, for his wise and just recommendations for minor but important revisions and additions just before the book was put to press. And, finally, I am grateful for the careful attention given the manuscript by Bowker staff editors, Judy Garodnick and Filomena Simora.

CURTIS G. BENJAMIN

Weston, Connecticut
September 1977

Introduction

In the autumn of 1961 I had the chance to spend several weeks touring Latin America with Curtis "Ben" Benjamin and Francisco Aguilera, a charming Latin American expert of the Library of Congress. We had been dispatched by Franklin Book Programs under a State Department contract to do a study of Latin American publishing as a basis for recommendations for U.S. programs in education, technical assistance, and cultural relations in that region. That was a long time ago, when I thought of myself as still filled with youthful vigor. I was a little concerned, however, as to whether Ben, a man 13 years older than myself, would be able to sustain so arduous a trip. We put in long days interviewing publishers and local officials, inspecting printing plants, visiting schools and universities, making exhausting parades of our limping Spanish. At the close of work each day we would repair to Ben's room for a "literary seminar," where a bottle of sour mash bourbon would appear. Dinner would follow at the Hispanic hour of nine or ten, and we would fall in bed by midnight.

But I needn't have worried. About seven in the morning, I would likely be awakened by a rap on the door, and a fresh and fully clad Ben would poke his head in to ask a question about notes he'd been working on for a couple of hours the previous night, after Aguilera and I had collapsed.

The whole trip was a wonderful experience, but the best part of it was to be in daily contact with the exuberant energy, the personal warmth, the eager curiosity, the perspicacious judgment, and the constructive devotion to the public interest that characterize Curtis Benjamin.

After an education at the universities of Kentucky and Arizona, and an early career that showed promise as a bookseller, playwright, stage director, and tenderfoot cowhand, Curtis Benjamin was drawn from an Arizona ranch by telegram, inviting him to apply for a vacant salesman's position in the Macmillan Company. The telegram was late reaching him down on the Mexican border, and by the time he had collected his gear and driven to New York in a Model T, the Macmillan job was filled. It may have been one of the best things that ever happened for the McGraw-Hill Book Company, for that is where he turned after the Macmillan disappointment. He was hired as a college traveler in 1928. Through the depression and war years he moved steadily up the ranks of that company until he became its president in 1946.

For the next twenty years, until 1966, he remained president or chairman of the board of the McGraw-Hill Book Company. Ben was always an expansionist, both in his publishing philosophy and in his drive for success, and those twenty years as head of a major book publisher during an era of industry growth gave him a marvelous opportunity. He was determined to prove that it was possible for a company to publish hundreds of books a year and still maintain the quality of its lists. He believed that with effective management to uphold editorial and production standards, the company could be expanded successfully into many new areas. If General Electric could operate profitably and maintain quality in some 50 or 60 subsidiaries or divisions, he argued, a publishing company ought to be able to operate 10 to 20 or even more market-oriented divisions. He still espouses this thesis, as can be seen throughout this book.

And his efforts succeeded. When he took over the McGraw-Hill Book Company, its annual revenues were under $10 million. Twenty years later they were well over $100 million—a more than tenfold increase. The pre-tax profits also had risen manyfold, to

$15.9 million. He always liked to see profits rise at a faster rate than sales.

But Ben's contribution to McGraw-Hill was not to be measured in dollars alone. In 1946, McGraw-Hill's book publishing operations were almost entirely concentrated in the field of technical works and college texts—primarily engineering, science, business, and related subjects. There was a small but active trade division and a quite small school division, serving only the vocational high school market. Though some McGraw-Hill books were exported, the only overseas subsidiary was in Great Britain, and no books were published abroad. Ben set out to make the company a comprehensive publisher, operating in all fields and throughout the world.

Through major acquisitions (including the Gregg Publishing Company, the Harper high school list, the Blakiston medical list from Doubleday, the Webster Publishing Company, and Shepard's Citations) and through internal developments, McGraw-Hill expanded into almost every area of publishing under Ben's leadership. Elementary, high school, and post-high school paraprofessional/technical publishing became areas of major strength, as did educational films correlated with basic texts—a pioneering concept of audio-visual supplements. Several important, monumental series, such as the MIT Radiation Laboratory Series, the National Nuclear Energy Series, and the Boswell Papers, were undertaken, in addition to more than 50 new, open-ended series of college and professional books. *The Encyclopedia of Science and Technology*, the *Encyclopedia of World Art*, and the *New Catholic Encyclopedia* were among the major undertakings he initiated.

All through the years, Ben gave special attention to McGraw-Hill's international operations. Exports were stepped up, and subsidiary companies in Australia, Mexico, and South Africa were added to those in Canada and Great Britain. These were charged not only with marketing U.S. editions abroad, but also with their own publishing programs. By the time of Ben's retirement, the international operations of the McGraw-Hill Book Company were worldwide, and were the company's fastest growing component. The knowledge of publishing and bookselling abroad gained by Ben in his travels to more than 40 foreign countries is reflected in this book.

Curtis Benjamin's contributions, however, were by no means confined to his own company. In the 1950s he served as a director of both book publishing trade associations then in existence, the American Book Publishers Council and the American Textbook Publishers Institute. He served a term as vice-president of the Institute and one as president of the Council, and initiated a movement that later led to their merger. He strongly believed that the book industry was tradition-ridden and should be reformed and modernized. He spent much time and energy at trying to improve its ways and its image—another facet of his career that is amply evident in several chapters of this book.

At the same time, while he was early aware of the great potentials of mechanized, computer-based systems for instruction and information transfer, he counseled a cautious approach to them. And he believed that when sound and profitable deployment of such systems came, it would come from publishers and not from the manufacturers and vendors of the hardware of such systems. Knowing that limited funds were available for the purchase of such systems, and being acutely aware of the conservative nature of the U.S. educational establishment, he took a dim view of the excitement over teaching machines and similar mechanical instructional gadgets that occurred in the 1960s. But he was not, and is not now, negative about the power and potentials of mechanical and electronic systems; he simply believes that the time has not come for book industry involvement with them in a big way. This attitude is reflected at several places in the chapters that follow.

From its founding, Ben was a member of Franklin Book Programs, the industry's nonprofit organization to aid publishing in developing countries, and served terms as a director and as treasurer. Throughout the decades-long process that led to the enactment of the Copyright Act of 1976, he was a strong voice of publishing, and from 1959 to 1965, and again in 1971–1972, he was chairman of the Book Industry Joint Committee on Copyright Problems.

He served the federal government as well, through membership on many committees and councils, such as the President's Science Advisory Committee, the National Science Foundation, the Atomic Energy Commission, the State Department, and the Office of Education, and also as member or chairman of U.S. delegations to UNESCO, and other international conferences on book-related matters. In all of these public activities, his complete devotion to the public interest was matched only by his complete conviction that this interest was usually best served by responsible private action.

As president of the American Book Publishers Council, he appointed its first committee on book marketing—a move that disquieted a number of his colleagues who wanted that organization to remain a cozy club where members could gather and talk to each other about the lofty nature of their occupation and its products. Being a homespun realist, he heartily disliked what he considered the froufrou and the publicity seeking that went along with popular book publishing. He never attended a literary luncheon or cocktail party if he could possibly avoid it. As the reader will see, he considered this to be a harmful narcissistic characteristic of the industry.

After his retirement from the McGraw-Hill Book Company, he served for a time as a director and for ten years as a consultant to the overall McGraw-Hill Corporation. Of this period, he devoted almost two years to an intensive study that contributed to the establishment of a staff office for corporate planning and development at McGraw-Hill, Inc. But the time finally came when he retired completely. It has been remarked that "complete retirement" meant that he might leave his office as early as three on a sunny Friday afternoon in May.

But the energy and interests are unending, and at the time of writing, Ben, as an independent consultant, has been retained by the Association of American Publishers to advise on creating a center for education for book publishing. And that, in a sense, is what this book is about: summarizing a lifetime of experience in the publishing of books of every kind, everywhere. Publishing has greatly changed since the late 1950s, when, as president of both the McGraw-Hill Book Company and the American Book Publishers Council, Ben was a prime mover at its very center; but the changes have been for the most part along lines he foresaw and promoted. What he has here written both reflects experience of the past and provides insights for the future.

DAN LACY

New York 1977

1

A Problem of Identity

It is difficult to define book publishing in a way that is satisfactory to those who are in it, much less to those who know little or nothing about it. Is it a profession? Or a trade? Or, in a broader sense, an industry? It all depends, of course, on who is doing the defining, or on what kind of book publishing is under consideration, or on the particular point of reference to the complex, hybrid enterprise that book publishing really is. But, regardless of a proper definition, it is the combination of professional and commercial activities that makes book publishing so attractive to so many of us who know and love it as an occupational way of life. Indeed, this is what attracted most of us to it in the first place.

The publisher—the organizational person at the top who coordinates the two kinds of activity—is the true occupational hybrid. A wise colleague of mine likes to say, "The best way to make a good publisher is to add the dollar sign to a good editor." This is the easiest way, to be sure. A harder way is to add editorial knowledge and perception to a good sales manager, or to another kind of specialist from the business side. The latter has been done with notable success, but not often. At any rate, the blending seems to be a requisite of success in the making of a true-blue publisher.

Until the end of the eighteenth century in the Western world, the book publisher was a tradesman, plain and simple. Usually he was a bookseller who had editions printed for sale principally by his own shop. Occasionally he was also a craftsman who operated his own printing press in a back room of his bookshop. (In Colonial America this combination was considered degrading because bookselling as an occupation was much more genteel than printing/publishing.[1]) But, as time went by, the trade and craft functions were left by the wayside, and the publisher emerged as a stripped-down catalytic agent of the author, the printer, and the bookseller. His role was to serve all their interests and his own as well. His task was to come up consistently with products that would have cultural or intellectual or educational worth and would, at the same time, be profitable to all concerned. Not an easy one by any means!

By the middle of the nineteenth century, most American publishing houses had sloughed the retailing function. The label "Publisher & Bookseller" was rarely seen thereafter. By 1900 most houses had abandoned the printing function as well; industrial specialization had arrived, and they found it cheaper to buy milk than to operate a dairy. Moreover, many had learned that idle printing presses were a temptation to the cardinal sin of publishing—excessively large runs that result in serious losses from overstocks. The best way to resist this temptation, they reasoned, was to remove it completely. So the printing plants were sold off or leased, and printing was farmed out by competitive bids or long-term contracts.

Thus the book publisher was at once both reduced and elevated to an entrepreneurial role—to being an intermediary between the world of intellect and culture and the world of commerce and industry. It became a role that, even today, is not clearly understood by the general public. (How often one hears, "Now, tell me, just what does a publisher do?") And, as suggested at the outset, many publishers still have trouble deciding just what their occupation really is.

With the sloughing of the "trade" coloration, it was natural that book publishers would find it satisfying to elevate, even to aggrandize, the nature of the publishing enterprise and of its product—and, by extension, themselves. Those in belletristic publishing often looked upon themselves as impressarios, organizers and purveyors of artistic works for the cultured public. This exaltation of the occupational status and societal role of publishers reached its zenith in the first half of the present century. In the United States, it came in an era of many individually or family owned houses, and it gave rise to personality cults in the industry. It was a time when giants bestrode the book world, such people as George Doran, Nelson Doubleday, Horace Liveright, Charles Scribner II, Alfred Harcourt, Donald Brace, Henry Laughlin, Warder Norton, Blanche and Alfred Knopf, Cass Canfield, Max Schuster, Harold Guinzburg, and others whom their colleagues and the press properly glamorized and exalted. These people were the image-makers of their industry, and they raised the image to a level of intellectual and societal consequence that was far above the commercial base on which it stood. Several of these image-makers had, of course, built upon solid foundations erected by their predecessors in the previous three decades of the preceding century. That was a period in which a few earlier and now-legendary giants had emerged from the earth, some with very earthy habits and vigor. Among them were the Harper brothers, W. H. Appleton, George Palmer Putnam, J. B. Lippincott, Frank H. Dodd, Henry Houghton, Charles Scribner, Henry Holt, Frank N. Doubleday, and George P. Brett. They were the "founding fathers" and they put down solid bases for the next generation to build upon.

So it was that book publishing came, after the turn of the century, to look upon itself as a profession, an elegant profession, and no doubt about it. (A well-known English publisher epitomized the spirit of the era in the title of a book about book publishing produced in 1959: *An Occupation for Gentlemen.*[2]) All this was somewhat narcissistic, of course, but it did firmly establish the book publisher as an entrepreneur of the intellect and a purveyor of knowledge and culture.

Naturally, the early decades of the twentieth century are now thought of as the Golden Age of publishing—as a time when publishers of refined taste and sure discrimination published only books of high literary and intellectual merit. The folklore of that era is now accepted as fact and truth, and perhaps it does represent the romantic truth, if not the actual fact, about the best of our industry in that period. In any case, the folklore still gets in the way of a generally satisfactory definition of book publishing as it is practiced today. And, of course, that particular Golden Age, like other shining eras of the past, did not last long. Marked changes would occur in the 1960s and the 1970s, of which the most important was a belated and reluctant recognition of the fact that book publishing is basically a business enterprise.

Many publishers resisted the idea that, as their industry grew in size, the heads of houses had to grow in their knowledge of modern business methods, including administration, finance, production, marketing, product distribution, customer relations, and personnel management and training. But gradually the industry accepted the idea that a mastery of the central editorial function was not enough, that more than a smattering of knowledge of the ancillary management functions was necessary for success under increasing competition for the book buyer's dollar. Thus the harm done by the industry's aggrandizement of itself and its product and by its often professed disdain for grubbing commercialism has been largely, but not wholly, remedied in recent years.

So it remained for a leading publisher of the "new school" to give, in 1977, a modern but still confounded definition of book publishing under the rubric "The Accidental Profession." In his introduction of a report to the AAP (Association of American Publishers) on the urgent need for more and better education and training for people in the industry, Samuel S. Vaughn, president of Doubleday Publishing Company, wrote:

> To those of us who practice publishing, it is a curious, crazy, beloved, frustrating, maddening, imperfect, demanding, compelling . . . business or art or profession or job. Which is it? It is, at its best, a vocation.

> And it is one in which most people find themselves by accident . . . or at least by indirection, chance, family, or other quirky connections. It has long seemed (erroneously) a perfect refuge for those who "love to read," and/or wanted to write, or who didn't know what to do. Not more than a few publishers ever prepared themselves consciously for a life in publishing.[3]

To this rather fanciful but sharply accurate definitional statement, Mr. Vaughn added an equally valid contrapuntal observation:

> The accidental nature of publishing contributes to its spontaneity, liveliness, charm, rewards and broken fortunes. No line of this report argues for educational improvements so systematized as to preclude the presence of the brilliant drop-in or to ward off the gifted and intuitive drop-out or to diminish the delight of the man or woman who wakes up one day and realizes that he/she has found not just a job but a lifelong commitment.

> This report does argue that accident, aimlessness, misunderstanding, or indirection is not good enough. And it is costly.[4]

Just why it is costly, and just how the wayward nature of the industry harms the people who are in it, will be noted in appropriate places as this critique progresses. Meanwhile, those who like to define book publishing as a profession will do well to ponder another statement from the AAP report quoted above:

> Publishing is popularly referred to as a profession. Though there are professionals at work in book publishing, the industry meets none of the classical standards of a profession, in neither the formal nor the admiring sense. There are no formal educational requirements, no set apprenticeship, no code of ethics or practice or means of exclusion or expulsion.

> Much of this is to the good; it keeps publishing wide open and free, so that anyone that sets up shop and somehow distributes a book has the right to be called a publisher. At the same time there is reason to consider whether the industry could not become more professional, without loss of charm or freedom or its attractive, random qualities.[5]

Thus speak the leaders of the latest generation of publishers. They speak very cogently and directly to the point.

2

The Sirenic Attractions

 $\mathbf{W}$ hy do people go into book publishing? How do they get there? Once there, why do they stay? Such questions are asked thousands of times, and there are as many answers, almost, as there are instances of their asking. The last question in particular comes often and naturally to the minds and lips of young people who have reached critical points in their starting years in the business. "Why in hell do I stay in this job?" "Isn't there another way to earn a better living?" "Where can I possibly go from here?" Often there is good reason, indeed, for such questioning.

When I was a young sprout in the business, a college traveler in the late 1920s, I often asked myself these questions, and as often heard them discussed in bull sessions with my peers and betters. Many a midnight, after-poker collocation on the subject would end with a wisesaw uttered by one of the senior members of our fellowship. Pulling sagely at the stem of his pipe, he would remark, "Well, there's one thing you can say for sure about the book business—it's not really good enough to stay in, but it's hardly bad enough to quit." Most of us agreed with this assessment, and we did stay in the business, for better or for worse. Still, all of us had heard that Frank N. Doubleday was the only U.S. publisher who ever had made even a modest fortune in the business, and we knew that his son Nelson was the only book publisher of that day who owned a yacht. We had secret hopes, but little cause to expect such high financial reward.

Things have changed considerably, to be sure, since that day. Book publishing by past standards has become "big business," yet it is not, even today, an occupation that anyone would choose for making a large fortune. Compared with many other industries, its starting salaries are low and its final and highest financial rewards usually are modest. (A 1975 study of executive compensation in 19 U.S. industries discovered that publishing ranked the lowest of all.) Decidedly, it still is not an occupation for any young person who has a yen for getting rich quickly.

One of the reasons why initial salaries in the book business are low is the competition for starting jobs. This arises mostly from the romanticized attraction of the industry for many young people just out of college. Every summer scores of eager graduates flock to New York and to the few other major publishing centers, each yearning to become a part of the glamorized literary scene. Most of them have been editors of, or contributors to, campus publications. And almost all of them want to be trade book editors; they have little or no interest in any other kind of work or in any other area of publishing. (Most of them emphatically disdain textbook departments where jobs are more frequently available.) Very few are willing to consider the advantages and potentials of a secretarial job, even when they are advised that it could be the best path for learning and advancement in most houses. High-grade secretarial skills are always wanted and appreciated at the top levels of administration and editorial management, and the combination of such skills with knowledge learned at the elbow of an experienced editor or manager is usually the quickest way to a high-level position. Yet, sadly enough, many young people are fearful of starting their business careers as secretaries. What a pity!

Further, many of the seekers of first jobs in book publishing are only looking for subsistence until they have written the great American novel or play. They beg for starting jobs at almost any wage. Naturally, this perennial supply of new recruits, this attraction of so many bright and hopeful youngsters, more interested in the job than the pay, has a depressing effect on the wage scale for beginners. And some of these eager beginners who actually have little to offer stay in low-paying, pedestrian jobs year after year, clinging not so much to their jobs as to their dreams of fortuitous advancement into a glittering career. Not many of them ever make it, but enough do to keep many other newcomers dreaming.

Other young people come into publishing at the beginner's level but with more maturity and less enchantment. They are less starry-eyed because they are seeking a second career—budding authors who have failed to flower, reporters who cannot live with the pressure of deadlines, teachers who have found that both kids and principals get on their nerves, librarians who love books but find life dull among the stacks, advertising neophytes who do not like the fast pace, salespeople who have found no satisfaction in selling insurance or men's underwear, et alii. They are the "drop-ins" with which the industry is loaded, and most of them come from low-paying jobs, attracted to book publishing as a supposedly genteel and slow-paced occupation. So they, too, are not demanding in the matter of compensation. Some of them, the journalists and the still-budding authors, often look upon their new employment as part-time work as they continue their creative writing. Not a few of the men among them continue to be partially supported by wives who are working in higher-paying industries until that best-seller or smash-hit play is finally produced. It is this attraction of creative-minded people—and of others who seek a relatively relaxed, intellectually related way of life—that gives book publishing such a large quantum of employees who turn into nomads within their industry.

Surely, there is no other type of business—save advertising, perhaps—where employees float about so freely and easily and perpetually from one house to another. Many competent people move about restlessly, like players in a game of "musical chairs." Others are pushed about because they are only marginally interested and do not give their best to their jobs. They move up, down, and sideways, but many of them stay on and on in the book business, trapped by its sirenic attractions. This occupational life-style is, of course, as harmful to their employers as to the floaters themselves. Still, it has been accepted by a large part of the industry as an inevitable and ineffable peculiarity of book publishing. Actually most of the floaters on the editorial side are seeking intellectual satisfaction without coming to terms with the industry's commercial demands.

It goes without saying that top management—meaning the heads of our publishing houses—must accept full responsibility for tolerating the high incidence of low-paid, floating personnel that characterizes both the editorial and sales staffs of our industry. Too many of us have been willing to hire and to maintain low-paid employees simply because so many marginally competent people are willing to work at salary levels that keep our payrolls down. This none of us likes to admit because it is both a discredit to us as businesspeople and a blight on the economy of our industry. Notwithstanding the harm done, most of us do tolerate a large quantum of low-performing personnel year after year without end. We excuse ourselves by saying that ours is an unordinarily humane kind of business, that we are an industry with a heart. This may well be so, but certainly our behavior butters no carrots, either for ourselves or for our first-rate editorial and sales personnel.

On the other side of publishing—the business side—starting salaries and higher pay are nearer industrial norms, but still somewhat on the low side. Operating as it does, our industry simply cannot afford higher pay scales on either side. Our chronic failure to work at upgrading and holding employees who have come to us by "accident, aimlessness, misunderstanding, or indirection" takes a serious economic toll that most publishers prefer not to think about, much less to try to correct. Our casual and unprofessional view of the need for formalized in-house training and professional education was described by the Education for Publishing Committee as being "short-sighted, expensive, and corrosive." This censorious description was then amplified:

> Let us extend the caution into a criticism: for an industry whose lifeline is linked to the world of education, we have been appallingly apathetic about our own. . . . For decades, attempts to educate

people for publishing have been, with a few notable exceptions, sporadic, scattered, hit-and-miss. The occasional seminar, the odd paper, cooperation with one or two institutions of higher learning.[1]

The notion that publishing is too arcane, too subtle, too elevated to be learned, except through the pores and by exposure to our stars is snobbery and laziness. Too few publishing people even read the too few books on publishing.[2]

And regarding the value and cost of in-house training and educational assistance for drop-in employees:

The way in and up the usual routes takes too long. . . . So, any consideration of the cost of helping people to become better publishers must be viewed against the hidden costs of the loss in people and in publishing investment. *Whatever* training costs, whatever educational assistance costs, it is a bargain.[3]

Now, as to the cost of supporting the "musical chairs" employment syndrome of the industry, the report cites estimates that were published in the February 1975 issue of *Nation's Business*:

A review of hiring costs can be a real eye-opener. . . . Estimated cost of hiring a secretary, $1,500; an accountant at $2,965; a "low-level" low-manager at $11,050; a "mid-level" mid-manager at $18,300.[4]

These are estimates of direct costs only; the hidden costs of lost time and decreased productivity probably are two or three times larger at each level. Small wonder, then, that the members of the AAP Education for Publishing Committee were so much disturbed by the findings and conclusions of their two-year study. And how sad that one section of the report reckoned: "By any measure, America's publication education is, in comparison with Germany, England, Japan, and France, that of an underdeveloped country."[5]

But the American book industry's waywardness in this debilitating matter is not beyond reform. In fact, we already have evidence that the work of the AAP committee has aroused the industry generally, and that reform is under way in many houses, both large and small. Yes, we are undoubtedly beginning to realize that long lines of applicants waiting at our doors for glamorous, low-paying jobs are not as providential as they appear to be.[6]

More will be said later about certain other debilitating customs and ailments of the book industry. Meanwhile, just what, specifically, are the offsetting attractions that bind so many people to an occupation that offers such unattractive financial rewards?

As noted at the outset, the basic attraction—the combination of commercial and intellectual or educational interests—offers the job seeker an unusual occupational opportunity. And once on the job, the beginner does indeed find many satisfactions of a kind that can be found in very few other industries or professions. This is why most people in book publishing, though they are an underpaid and restless and plaintive lot, seem seldom to think seriously of seeking any other kind of employment. How often one hears: "There's something about the book business that makes it a lively and engrossing place to work." I find it pleasurable, even exciting, to describe these occupational charms.

First, book publishers have the cardinal satisfaction of knowing that they are helping to supply humankind's greatest need, the universal need for knowledge and enlightenment, without which no person can act wisely and justly. They supply, also, the needs for entertainment, for inspiration, and for the enrichment and guidance of the lives of all who can read. It was Thoreau who once exclaimed, "How many a man has dated a new era in his life from the reading of a book!"

Second, publishers know that they are dealing in the stuff with which Western civilization has been built. With Carlisle they believe that "in books lies the soul of the whole of past time." Accordingly, they can feel that they have a part in keeping alive the records of the world's intellectual, cultural, and material attainments.

Further, publishers can feel, in a corollary way, that they are producing products of the mind that will have lasting value. Today's newspapers are quickly read and promptly discarded; magazines are usually partially read and kept for a few weeks or months. Both have little more than transient interest and are never reprinted. But books have, most of them, much longer lives; usually they are read, and then kept on handy shelves for several months or several years. Indeed, some books live for decades, even for centuries. Hence book publishers can relish the often-quoted classical statement by Clarence Day: "The world of books is the most remarkable creation of man; nothing else that he builds ever lasts. Monuments fall, civilizations grow old and die out. After an era of darkness, new races build others; but in the world of books are volumes that live on, still young and fresh as the day they were written; still telling men's hearts of the hearts of men centuries dead." Inspired by such thoughts as these, any true-blue publisher can always hope, in time, to publish at least a few books that will be read and reread with pleasure and profit long after the publisher is dead and buried.

Further, publishers are always aware that they are living on the frontier of the mind and the spirit. They know that they must keep closely attuned to the changing and generative affairs of their time—to all the cultural, educational, political, and commercial advances of the world about them. President Franklin D. Roosevelt put this matter succinctly in a letter of congratulations to Harper & Brothers on the occasion of that house's one hundred twenty-fifth anniversary: "There are few businesses that are so intimately interwoven with the national fabric as a publishing house."

Operating as they do, always on the advancing frontier of ideas and events, publishers know the excitement of an explorer of the new and unknown. They look constantly for fresh opportunities for the extension and improvement of their lists. Alert publishers always try to be riding the right wave, and they can try occasionally to start their own waves of the future. What elation they must feel when they succeed at that!

Concomitantly, alert publishers are also the constant searchers and discoverers of new literary talent. And in some cases they are the refiners, even the molders, of discovered fresh talent. The publishers who do discover a latent talent and nurse it along to matured success experience real elation. Then they feel that they are functioning in a truly creative way, and this every publisher considers to be the *summum bonum* of one's occupational life.

In addition, publishers have the great satisfaction of knowing that they help to carry on the tradition of freedom of thought and freedom of expression, the cornerstones upon which any democratic society is built. Book publishers have always been in the front line of battle against censorship; they know and support the historic power of books in the never-ending struggle against any sort of oppression of the mind or the spirit.

In quite another way, publishers enjoy the intrepid excitement of being always the gambler. They must constantly pit their wits and judgment (and luck) against the uncertainties and vagaries of the public's prevailing interests and tastes. In doing so, they always try, of course, to reduce their risks to odds that can be calculated or sensed in one way or another. Still, they know that risk taking is congenital to their business, that they must habitually expect success but be prepared for failure. In short, a publisher must learn to live with risk and chance, to exalt success and discount failure, to be forever the optimist, certain that tomorrow's gain will far exceed yesterday's loss. Those who cannot attune their psyches to this attitude will never be able to enjoy the book business as it should be enjoyed.

Finally, book publishers have the crowning good fortune of dealing constantly with the creation of new products. This serves to refresh the mind and the spirit, season after season, year after year. The building of each season's list is, in fact, a process of generation and renewal—an endless procession of new books and revised editions, each of which is a fresh and different venture, each holding its own peculiar essence and promise. Naturally, this process of constant change and renewal leaves no room for monotony or boredom; neither does it permit complacency or smugness. On the contrary, it assures that the alert book publisher need never know a dull day.

3

Authors and Publishers:
An Uneasy Symbiosis

Although we publishers have an inordinately high-minded view of our "occupation for gentlemen," it must be admitted that a shadow of distrust has always hung over the printer/publisher as a businessperson. Down through the ages we have suffered a public reputation for sharp practices, and even today it can be assumed, I believe, that the average person looks upon all book publishers with at least a modicum of suspicion or distrust. Sadly, but naturally enough, this traditional view has been nurtured through the centuries by disgruntled authors who like to lambaste their publishers, often publicly and shrilly, for all sorts of real or fancied wrongs.

Dryden accused his publisher of having "two left legs and Judas-colored hair." Coleridge called publishers "cormorants in the Tree of Life," and added, "Let authors content themselves by saying . . . publishers are greedy and self-satisfied. Their literacy and efficiency are not up to their appetites." Both James Boswell and Robert Burns bitterly accused their publishers of mean and dilatory business practices—accusations that appeared to be fully justified in both cases. (Burns was particularly vociferous in criticizing his two printers/booksellers, though the first of them, William Creech, became a magistrate and was Lord Provost of Edinburgh late in life, and the second was the same William Smellie who wrote, edited, and printed the first edition of the *Encyclopaedia Britannica* as almost a one-man production. Both Creech and Smellie were apprentice-trained printers who became self-educated scholars. Being eighteenth-century Scotsmen who operated with stringently limited capital, they simply hated to give up money.)

The English philosopher John Locke complained in more general but no less bitter terms:

> Books seem to me to be pestilent things, and infect all that trade in them . . . with something very perverse and brutal. Printers, binders, sellers, and others that make a trade and gain out of them have universally so odd a turn and corruption of mind that they have a way of dealing peculiar to themselves, and not conformed to the good of society and the general fairness which cements mankind.

Somewhat later, Lord Byron's publisher, John Murray, gave the poet a finely bound copy of the Bible; Byron thereupon sought out the passage "Now Barabbas was a robber," crossed out the word "robber," inserted the word "publisher," and sent the copy back to Murray.

With all this classical evidence as background, it is easy to understand why, for almost two centuries, all the world has chuckled knowingly over reproductions of Rowlandson's droll but poignant caricature of the smug, fat publisher/bookseller listening disdainfully to the desperate plea of his tense, starving author. A truly drawn likeness, surely, of your typical publisher as Scrooge!

There must have been ample cause, certainly, for all this complaint against printers and publishers. Beyond doubt many printers-*cum*-publishers were guilty of sharp or downright dishonest practices in dealing with their authors. But it is also true that many publishers have been unjustly blamed and vilified by unsuccessful authors for the failure of their books and for the general unhappiness of the writer's lot. This is not surprising because most writers, like other creative people, have ingrained, high-level egos to support; hence they are quickly and deeply offended by failure. Their publishers are, of course, the most convenient and natural targets for blame. Blame so placed has become an occupational blemish that publishers have learned to expect and to accept philosophically. It seems to be a natural consequence of the symbiotic nature of the book world—of authors and publishers having to live together in close associations that are not always happy or mutually beneficial.

But it must not be thought that authors and publishers, having separate and selfish interest on each side, are natural foes. Not so at all, for actually they have more to pull them together than to split them apart. Neither should it be thought that the one is more put upon than the other. In actual fact, the popular stereotype of the poor and cheated author lost all semblance of validity many years ago. In most book publishing agreements, the modern author (at least the modern American author) has the better deal, which is to say that he stands to gain more in royalty than the publisher can gain in profit. And it usually works that way, as is evidenced by the fact that almost every reputable publishing house in America annually pays authors' royalties that are considerably larger than the amount of its own before-tax profit. (This is so in trade book publishing in particular, where a successful book often gives the author an income that is two or three times larger than the publisher's profit.)

Further, all reputable publishers have long since ceased the conventional practice of withholding the payment of royalties for unconscionably long periods of time. Authors are now paid promptly and fully—or at least as promptly as computer-based accounting systems can grind out statements and write checks that are untouched by human brains and hands. Thus the days are gone when publishers customarily and callously used their authors' capital for many months of each fiscal year.

Yet every publisher still has a share of unhappy authors who, like Dryden and Coleridge, are ready to level charges of incompetence or knavery or both. They are the ones, usually, whose books have been economic failures. With them the rub comes in the difference between their situation and that of publishers. The publisher can always balance winners against losers—one best-seller or a successful backlist title will offset the losses on several failures. Unfortunately, most authors cannot enjoy this balancing-out effect—alas, they must live with the bitterness of individual failures. It seems inevitable, then, that publishers will continue to be damned by disappointed authors and will have to bear the brunt of public suspicion as long as writers write for livelihood and books are printed for profit.

Here it should be noted that an author's dissatisfaction is occasionally exacerbated by owing the publisher an unearned balance of a cash advance that was made against royalty before publication of a commercially unsuccessful book. Indeed, this unhappy situation can cause lasting enmities between authors and publishers, for often the publisher considers an advance to be a loan the author is obligated to repay. And, unfortunately, publishing contracts are not always explicit on the question of repayment of an unearned balance. Nor, except in trade book publishing, has the industry developed a generally accepted custom for dealing with the matter. So some cases are dealt with on a catch-as-catch-can basis, and far too many of these are handled in arbitrary ways by "the business office." Small wonder that they do lead, now and then, to deeply hurt feelings and alienated affections.

What can be said of the looseness with which this delicate matter is handled in some publishing houses? First, it is inexcusable on the part of both the publisher and the author. Both should squarely face the possibility of failure and insist that, in every contract in which an advance is involved, the author's responsibility for a possibly unearned debit is explicitly stated. (Nowadays, most trade book contracts do specify that repayment of an unearned advance is not expected, except in case the author fails to deliver a publishable manuscript as agreed.) Further, the publishing house should recognize its implicit involvement in the author's risk taking. In making an advance of a specified amount, the publisher tacitly signifies a belief that enough copies of the author's book can be sold to generate sufficient royalty income to cover that amount. Accordingly, the house should feel its full share of responsibility for the plight of an author who becomes stuck with an unearned balance. Certainly the company is an accessory to, if not a partner in, the crime of failure. For this reason alone the publisher should always be lenient with an indebted author, and especially with one whose publishing contract has not dealt specifically with the question of repayment.

The problems of the failed book would not be so difficult if it were only the bad books that fail to sell. But as every publisher knows, good books—books of high literary or scholarly or intellectual merit—fail as often, if not more often, than do books of questionable merit. Often a book of high intrinsic merit will fail in the marketplace because its subject is too narrow or too esoteric to attract more than a handful of readers. Others fail because their treatment of the subject is too erudite and profound for wide readership. Still others fail because the timing of publication is unfavorable—perhaps two or three other recent books on the same subject have sated the literary or topical appetite of possibly interested readers. For these and other similar reasons, many good books have always suffered grievously high rates of economic failure; and often the better the book, the worse the failure. The publisher, being the one who decides what will sell well enough to justify publication, should accept a large share of the blame in every case of such failure. At any rate, the publisher certainly has a special obligation to the author of a failed book of high quality, and any resulting financial problem should be dealt with accordingly.

The foregoing preachment is not intended to imply that a publisher should hesitate to take calculated risks on books of such high quality or of such specialized content that they may be unprofitable. Rather, it is intended to suggest that publishers should always be cautious and prudent in their prepublication dealings with the authors of such books. Then is the time when due care should be taken that both sides are conditioned to the possibility, or probability, of commercial failure. Thus, if failure does come, the blow will have been cushioned. Then both parties to the flunk can relax with a feeling of "good try" satisfaction. The author's ego has been massaged by seeing his or her distinguished work in print; the publishing house has added another succès d'estime to its list. Indeed, the publisher occasionally may even feel a sense of elation, for it is a fact that true-blue publishers often love their failures as much as or more than their successes.

Another time-honored artifice of ethical dealing in book publishing often causes unhappiness among authors. This is the insistence that a manuscript must be submitted to only one publisher at a time. Thus, the author may not shop around, but must send the manuscript to a selected publisher who is assumed to have the exclusive right of acceptance or rejection. This means that the author must wait patiently for the publisher to make a decision, which often takes several weeks or even a few months. If the selected publisher rejects the manuscript, the author can then—and only then—submit it to another house and wait again. If there are two, three, or more rejections (a not uncommon experience by any means), the author must submit and wait again, and maybe yet again. Thus the procedure can become painfully strung out, and the author may have to spend many, many months, or even a few years, in trying to find a publisher. Further, the procedure deprives the author of the possible benefit of competitive offers, which means, of course, that there is no free market for authors' wares. Moreover, most beginners are required to pledge submission of their next manuscript before the contract for publication of the one in hand is signed.

Many people, and especially new writers, find it hard to understand and accept the *de rigueur* nature of this publishing practice. It appears to be rigged for the publisher's benefit and hence unfair to the author—so much so, indeed, that some established authors and their agents have begun to rebel against the practice.[1] Still, given the imbalance in the supply and demand of manuscripts, and considering the costs of editorial screening and selection, it is the only basis on which many publishers—and smaller ones in particular—can operate. Since both the sales and the profit incomes from the average book are low, the publisher cannot afford the considerable cost of reviewing and providing critical evaluation of a manuscript that may go to any one of several other houses. Moreover, the report on a promising manuscript might not be as critical as it should be if the editor knows that a competitor, reading the manuscript concurrently, may land its author with a less critical report. So, rightly or wrongly, publishers usually insist on the right of exclusive review with the understanding that a manuscript will be theirs if it is found acceptable and if reasonable terms for its publication are offered.

It should be noted, however, that the publisher's own foot is not pinched by the same shoe when it comes to selling secondary rights in a published book. With a successful title in hand, the publisher usually opens the bidding for reprint, book-club, motion-picture, and magazine serialization rights. Competitive offers will be invited in each area, and then the author's approval of the most lucrative offer will be sought. Indeed, the author (or the author's agent) often works closely and happily with the publisher in exploiting all competitive possibilities, and no one appears to see anything wrong with the robustness of this open competition. Rather, both sides seem to agree that this is the best way simply because it is the way that works best. Thus questions of policy easily give way to pragmatism, and everybody is happy except the buyers of secondary rights.

Now, having elaborated some of the uneasy aspects of author-publisher relations that have, rightly or wrongly, gained public credence, I should balance the picture by indicating just why authors and publishers have more to pull them together than to split them apart.

It is a sure—but not conspicuous—fact that many, many authors have found deep and lasting satisfaction with their publishers. Indeed, a good number of close personal friendships, cemented by mutual trust and respect, have been notable in the annals of book publishing. Kipling's deep admiration and affection for Frank Doubleday, Mencken's regard for and loyalty to Alfred Knopf, and Steinbeck's confidence and trust in Pascal Covici—these are but three of many classical examples of author-publisher closeness and fidelity that are well known in publishing circles.[2] Many similar relationships have occurred in educational and professional book publishing, but they go unsung, of course—even within the book industry. Alas, happy relationships are rarely noticed publicly in a world that seems to prefer bad news to good news. And it seems that bad blood between author and publisher often makes newspaper headlines, never mind how petty and unimportant the quarrel may be.

It is a cliché to say that publishing a book is a partnership venture, but it is nonetheless true. Or, certainly, that is the way it always should be. The author is, to be sure, the generative and dominant partner, something that the wise publisher never forgets. Yet, the publisher usually plays an important part, first in helping the author to do the best work possible, and then in presenting it to the public in the best possible form.

In the generative phase, the publisher can give critical assistance in major matters of structure, substance, and style, and also frequently can help the author to focus properly on the reader for whom the book is intended. This appears to be a simple matter, but it is troublesome to many writers. The author's natural tendency is to try to appeal to the widest possible audience, or maybe to several different audiences, imagining thousands of readers who do not exist in reality. The publisher, keeping an eye on a known type of reader and a discrete book market, often can help inexperienced authors to overcome this conceptual fault.

Further, at the manuscript-reading stage, the publisher (or the house's assigned editor) can question what appear to be unnatural characterizations, unwarranted exaggerations, unfair prejudices, invalid comparisons, illogical reasoning, precarious judgments, unsupportable conclusions, and dubious inferences or deductions. And, of course, editors help authors to deal with important trivia such as factual errors, incorrect usage, ambiguities, solecisms, inconsistencies, misinterpretations, non sequiturs, wrong references, and awkward circumlocutions. Most authors are deeply grateful for this kind of technical assistance—it relieves them of a nagging worry about the imperfections of their work.

Later, at the production stage, authors are always grateful for assistance with the tasks of proofreading, indexing, and compiling bibliographic references. Often they will have reached a state of mental exhaustion before these exacting tasks are finished. Thus they find themselves in need of psychic support, and this, too, is customarily supplied by their partner, the publisher.

Finishing a manuscript and seeing it through to the bound-book state is truly a nerve-wracking experience for almost all authors. But most of them come through it with a pronounced sense of gratitude for the "value added" that the editorial process has provided. And usually they have formed a feeling of respect, if not friendship, for their partners. They have learned that the author-publisher relationship is a very special one—something like a marriage of minds in an intellectual/commercial endeavor. And there the happy alliance is likely to stay—unless, by chance, the book fails to sell. Such an event, as noted earlier, usually is the crucial test of the partnership. That is, alas, where the contrariety of the relationship so often sets in.

Almost a century ago, William Dean Howells, a successful editor as well as a highly regarded writer, summed up this contrariety in a comment that publishers like to quote to this day:

> I for one wish to bear witness to the constant good faith and uprightness of publishers. . . . It is true that publishers will drive a hard bargain when they can, or when they must, but there is nothing to hinder an author from driving a hard bargain, too, when he can, or when he must; and it is to be said of the publisher that he is always more willing to abide by the bargain when it is made than the author is, perhaps because he has the best of it. But he has not always the best of it; I have known publishers too generous to take advantage of the innocence of authors; and I fancy that if publishers had to do with any race less difficult than authors, they would have won a repute for unselfishness that they do not now enjoy.

This classical comment attests the fact that, though the book industry has changed a great deal over the past hundred years, the human nature of authors and publishers has changed not a whit.

4

The Genteel Art of Poaching, Keeping, and Losing Authors

In the genteel tradition of book publishing, no publisher ever steals another publisher's author. Indeed, if book publishers had a formalized canon of ethical conduct, its first commandment surely would be: "Thou shalt not covet thy competitor's author, neither shalt thou entice nor steal an author away." But in actuality this traditional adjuration has little force. In the real world, author stealing, like spouse stealing, is a common transgression; the unwritten law against it is far more honored in the breach than in the observance. Still, many publishers—and especially the few "of the old school" who are left—like to inveigh, both privately and publicly, against it. In most instances, their condemnations can be taken as no more than wishful self-delusion or bombast, or perhaps some of both.

This is, to be sure, harsh censure of professed righteousness; nevertheless it is merited. Anyone who has not actually experienced the stealing and enticing practices of the industry can verify the truth of the matter by reading a few of the many factual accounts of the vagaries of author-publisher relationships down through the years.[1] There one can find many cases of outright theft, and many more of cleverly devised enticements that cannot be so clearly recognized for what they really are. The enticements usually are masked by maneuverings that make it appear the pilfering publisher is innocent of wrongdoing and is merely opening the door to the author who has made a prior decision to move to another house.

The searcher of publishing history will even find a good number of cases of wholesale enticement of authors. For instance, when Alfred Harcourt, one of the most respected and successful publishers of our century, left Henry Holt and Company in 1919 to establish his own firm, he walked off with several of Holt's leading authors, including Dorothy Canfield Fisher, Walter Lippmann, Carl Sandburg, Louis Untermeyer and Joel Spingarn. He failed to ensnare Robert Frost only because the poet suspected a deception in Harcourt's intrigue with him. (In addition, Harcourt persuaded Donald Brace, Holt's production manager, to join him as a partner, and the two of them then enticed "Gus" Gehrs, Holt's potent sales manager, to come over to the new firm in that capacity.) Apparently, Harcourt had earlier made author purloining a regular practice at Holt, for Alfred Knopf, Sr., once wrote, "So Alfred [Harcourt]—and he told me this himself at the time—looked over his unfriendly competitor's list very carefully, picked out what he considered to be the two most promising young novelists on it, sent for them, and gave each the price he asked for coming over to Holt. Sinclair Lewis was one of the two—the other did not pay off. True, Lewis never appeared on the Holt list, but that was because Harcourt had set up his own firm before *Main Street* was written." Then Mr. Knopf added, "But a publisher seldom enjoys such sweet revenge. When we were a very young firm we didn't realize the extent of this poaching (actually it was rather uncommon before the First World War). We didn't watch our fences so to speak and thus lost in quick order, among others, Julian Huxley, Sheila Kaye-Smith, E. M. Delafield, Mary Borden, and H. M. Tomlinson."[2] All were well-established authors of the day.

Alfred Knopf was graduated from Columbia University in 1912, and soon thereafter obtained a job with Doubleday, Page and Company. He worked there for a year and a half, then joined Mitchell Kennerley, a well-known editor for John Lane of London, who had opened his own house in New York in 1904. There Knopf stayed for 14 months, when he decided to start out on his own with a capital of $3,000. In spite of his professed innocence of pre–World War I poaching practices, he soon managed to garner several excellent authors from the Doubleday, Page and Kennerley lists.

History repeated itself, in part, some 45 years later when Alfred A. ("Pat") Knopf, Jr., quit his father's firm and joined with Simon Michael ("Mike") Bessie of Harper and Hiram Haydn of Random House to found Atheneum Publishers. Within two years they managed to announce a list of ten or twelve distinguished authors. No one had to guess how it was managed that they appeared so soon on Atheneum's list.

Of single-author purloining, one can find many notable instances in the records of American publishing. As early as 1843, the Harper brothers easily induced historian Henry Prescott to move over from Little, Brown. Some years later, William James, in a quarrel with Holt, accepted an offer from Lippincott (but afterward returned to Holt). A less ancient instance was Random House's acquisition of *Ulysses* in 1931 after Viking refused to accept the terms set by Joyce's agent. Still later, Thomas Merton and others followed Robert Giroux from Harcourt, Brace when Giroux went from there to join Farrar, Straus in 1955.[3] And even later, McGraw-Hill took Vladimir Nabokov from Putnam in 1967 by offering him an attractive "package" deal, which included several of his early and little-known works that had not yet been translated from the Russian-language editions. This turned out to be a profitable grab, mainly because *Ada*, Nabokov's first full-length novel published by McGraw-Hill, was a worldwide bestseller.

All these reported examples of well-known breaches of the "no-poaching" canon of ethical publishing bring us squarely to the essential question: Just why should any author "belong," ethically or morally, to any *one* publishing house? The answer has to be equivocal.

As everyone in book publishing knows, Alfred Knopf has long claimed Willa Cather as his own—I had almost said his own creation. But the fact is that Miss Cather's talent and her first two manuscripts were discovered by Ferris Greenslet, Houghton Mifflin's stellar editor early in the century. He published her *O Pioneers* in 1913 and *My Antonia* two years later. Almost the same can be observed about Mr. Knopf's much-celebrated relationship with W. H. Hudson, whose *Green Mansions* was first published by Putnam in 1904 at a financial loss. But in 1914 Knopf had persuaded Kennerley to publish Hudson's *Adventures Among Birds*, so it should have been easy for him to persuade Hudson to come to him after his newly established firm had published a new and successful edition of *Green Mansions* with a laudatory introduction by John Galsworthy. Still it is a fact that Hudson was "acquired" by Knopf from another house. (If I seem to pick on Mr. Knopf, it is only because he is, beyond doubt, the most highly respected American publisher living today, and he is also the one who has, through the years, talked the most about his intimate relationships with his famous authors and about how other publishers had better stay away from them!)

So one has to say that an author "belongs" to a publisher because of having been helped well and treated fairly, and because a deep sense of loyalty has developed from long years of business relations that have turned into personal friendship and admiration. As noted earlier, there are in book publishing some celebrated instances of "belonging together," but they do not occur often, not by a long shot, as will be seen later.

A good number of even more recent, and hence more pertinent, cases of breaching the no-poaching canon could here be cited, but to do so would be imprudent. Assuredly, however, the poaching does continue, widely and year after year, in spite of the pretense that it is verboten among respectable publishers. So how do seasoned publishers deal with the reality that lies beneath the pretense? Well, they must again be philosophical, yet ever on guard against raiders of the fold (as Alfred Knopf professed not to be), knowing that one will surely come now and then, either stealthily in the night or boldly in broad daylight. And the publisher who is not too much the gentleman will be ready to return disfavors whenever tempting opportunities present themselves.

Willful desertion by successful and favored authors is another vexation that all publishers must expect from time to time. Such desertions are caused, more often than not, by temperamental flare-ups; in some cases they are, paradoxically, the result of too much success. Nearly always they spring from a wounding of the author's ego, but dissembling reasons often are given in explanation. In any case, the symbiotic love/hate relationship between the author and the publisher seems naturally to invite occasional alienation and defection. As Socrates observed, friendship often proves to be an unstable anchorage.

It was noted earlier that publishers expect to be blamed now and then for the failure of promising books. Also, they know that they will occasionally be blamed for not making a successful book even more successful—the author is sure that many more copies might have been sold had the publisher really appreciated the value of the book and done a proper job of promoting it. Hence it is to be expected that a dissatisfied author may decide to try another house the next time.

But what is not expected—and what hurts deeply when it comes—is the desertion of an author who has enjoyed success in a publisher's hands with several books through many years. Sadly enough, instances of such desertion are not at all infrequent. Some occur—and they are the saddest—when a long-established author begins to lose literary potency, as was the case of Sinclair Lewis when he blamed Harcourt, Brace for his fading success and left that firm after it had published more than a dozen bestsellers for him. Other desertions can occur when the writer comes to feel a sense of jadedness or personal pique in a close editorial relationship that has lasted too long. This was the feeling of Thomas Wolfe when he broke with Scribner after that house's premier editor, Maxwell Perkins, had wet-nursed his enormous talent through several very trying but highly successful years. Less celebrated cases of piqued desertion occur regularly but with scant notice.

Naturally, no house likes to lose an established author, yet the publisher usually does not try to hold authors against their will.

(Not unless there is a large debit in an author's royalty account, in which case the author may persuade another interested house to take over the obligation.) So the wise publisher does everything possible to keep authors happy and encouraged to get on with the work at hand. The publisher knows that the writer's impelling ego must be treated tenderly, that creative talent must be carefully nursed, and that in some cases the author's personal problems and business affairs must be looked after.[4] And the seasoned publisher knows that the matter must always be put directly and honestly to the restless author, just as Henry Holt put it to his fidgety friend William James in 1896:

> When an author is identified with a house, every new book of his gives the publisher a new chance to boom his old ones. If his books are scattered all over creation, he loses this benefit, and it is too important a one to lose. . . . Most publishers, like other men, are fools; and you authors, if you escape the fools, may be but lambs before the wolf. So your only safety is to find as nearly a regenerate and merciful wolf as you can, and then stick to him and let him take care of you.

For its veracity and force, that letter might have been written yesterday. Any budding publisher would do well to keep it at hand as a model statement of one of the enduring verities of the industry.

But a publisher who does have to argue with an unhappy or restless author should always remember that in the last analysis the publisher is on the receiving end and the authors are on the providing end—that the publishing house is there to serve the authors, not the other way around. In this relationship, the author's rights of choice are paramount; their work cannot morally be held as chattel against their will, even when there may be legitimate rights to do so. The wise and beholden publisher will constantly recognize the fact that authors, regardless of their frequent dissatisfactions, do provide the essential substance of the book industry. Hence, they and their works must be treated with due respect and deference. Indeed, just publishers should always bow—mentally at least—to every author they happen to meet.

5

The Problems
of Plagiarism,
Hoaxes, and Frauds

Another instance when the publisher's conscience and ethical values should always point the proper way is in dealing with cases of plagiarism, hoax, or fraud. Such cases occur quite regularly, even in the best publishing houses. Whenever they are at all serious in nature, or if they happen to involve public "personalities," they make good copy for press reports that often are grossly sensationalized. And, to be sure, they do serve woefully to magnify the popular view of the seamy side of publishing. Here, again, seasoned publishers know they must bear the inflamed odium patiently and philosophically, for there is really very little that they can do effectively to guard against being put upon or taken in by a careless or unscrupulous author.

What the public does not understand is that under the practicalities of manuscript review and editing procedures, none but the most obvious of plagiarisms is likely to be discovered before publication. Naturally, neither the manuscript reader nor the house editor can afford to research every passage or page of a manuscript to ensure that it is totally the work of the author. (It could be done, of course, but where would one find competent readers and editors who would take on the burden? And would book buyers want to pay the very large additional editorial cost?)

Actually, most plagiarisms are not substantial in size or substance, and all but a few of them are unintentional offenses, committed usually through carelessness or ignorance. Further, when an offense is discovered, the author almost always readily admits error and contritely accepts both blame and responsibility for the consequences—and the author is, indeed, fully responsible under the conditions of almost every book publishing contract. This is why most discovered instances of plagiarism can be dealt with without dispute. Minor infractions usually are forgiven after a due apology is made and a promise is given to correct the error in the next printing. But major infractions usually require the withdrawal of the edition, or the payment of a reasonable sum for damages, or both. In such cases, authors can, of course, be seriously hurt in their pocketbooks as well as their feelings. Hence, in each of these cases, the publisher should be lenient in keeping with the author's degree of culpability and the extent of the financial penalty incurred. As Shakespeare observed, the quality of mercy is "twice bless'd; it blesseth him that gives and him that takes."

It is much more difficult, both technically and morally, to deal with cases of literary hoaxes and frauds. Indeed, it is difficult to draw a hard line of distinction between the hoax and the fraud. But it is certain that the public is always ready to laugh *with* the publisher who has been deceived by a harmless hoax, and even more ready to laugh *at* one who has been deceived by a harmful fraud. (Could this be a knee-jerk response to what are taken as tables-turned situations?) As noted earlier, deceptions of both kinds have always been of morbid interest to the reading public and hence to the press. From the classical example of Macpherson's faked "translations" of the legendary Ossian poems in the 1760s down to the Clifford Irving "caper" of his purported "authorized" biography of the legendary Howard Hughes in this decade, many fraudulent literary works have attracted worldwide attention and front-page coverage. And, though falsely identified and dishonestly represented, some of them have had high literary merit or entertainment value. In fact, the spurious translation of the Ossian poems was probably the most widely admired of all romantic literary works produced in the English language in the eighteenth century, and it was indeed a masterpiece of poetic imagination and composition. And the fake was so skillful that it fooled even the literary astuteness of Dr. Samuel Johnson.

Of the more modern hoaxes, two notable ones are *Trader Horn* (or "The Life and Works of Alfred Aloysius Horn . . . taken down and here edited by Ethelreda Lewis") and Joan Lowell's *The Cradle of the Deep*. Both were published by Simon and Schuster in the late 1920s with that firm's characteristic flamboyant promotion, and both immediately became best-sellers. The former work had a glowing foreword by John Galsworthy and was a Literary Guild selection. Of the latter, the publisher said, "The book is so real and genuine and sincere and exciting that you can't let it go." The judges of the Book-of-the-Month Club innocently concurred with this statement and made the book their first selection. Even after each title in turn was exposed as a fake, it continued to sell briskly. A contemporary critic, Edward Uhlan, explained the unruffled popularity of the two books:

> Significantly enough, the disclosure that *Trader Horn* and *The Cradle of the Deep* were phonies didn't hurt their sale one iota. A charming faker is far more acceptable than an honest frump. The people who had handed over their money under the impression that they were buying the truth remained to cheer the fiction.

With all this in mind, the modern publisher is hard put, in all honesty, to form a hostile, or even a nugatory, attitude toward such works. Just where can a fine line be drawn between what is a dishonest but acceptable hoax and what is a dishonest and unacceptable fake? One test, obviously, is to ask whether the work has enough literary distinction or entertainment value to justify its publication, regardless of whether its identity and content have been faked. Another is to ask whether its publication is likely to cause mischievous or malicious harm to the welfare or good name of any person or class of persons. A third, and more easily determined, test is to ask whether the deception might seriously damage the publisher or the editor who is conned into accepting it under a false label. Still another, and perhaps the most difficult, test is to ask whether readers are likely to be deceived or misled in a harmful way. If the answers to all these questions are satisfactory, then the deception can be accepted and forgiven as a harmless hoax. Otherwise, neither the author nor the publisher (if the latter be privy to the spoof) can be excused from responsibility for any ill consequences of publication, either ethical or legal.

Now, what can be made of author Clifford Irving's famous "caper" with his publisher, McGraw-Hill, which narrowly missed being a successful literary hoax in the years 1971–1972? To those who know the full and true story of this shameful but fascinating misadventure, it is clear that Irving perpetrated a fraud that was criminal in nature and harmful in its consequence.[1] He deliberately set out to defraud his trusting publisher of a large sum of money—a sum that grew ever larger when it appeared that his imaginative, clever, and very skillfully executed plan of fraud seemed more and more likely to succeed. Also, he callously involved his wife and a friend as accomplices, and caused both of them to commit criminal acts for which they suffered humiliation and prison sentences. Yet Irving tried to pass off the whole thing as no more than a fatuity that, had it succeeded, would have harmed no one and might have produced an informative and entertaining book. Strange to say, this pretense was partly successful. With the help of an excited and sententious press, he became a clever and likable miscreant whose sin lay largely in being caught. Indeed, it seemed that, with the dénouement of the true story, the press and the general public had more sympathy for the defrauder Irving than for the defrauded publisher. By a curious perversion of fairness, many press reports insinuated McGraw-Hill's guilt of cupidity coupled with excessive credulity—if the publisher had not been so ready and eager to grab for a best-seller at a high price, the whole thing would not have happened. (Deplorably, a few other publishers fostered this view by censorious comments in the press.) This reaction of sympathy for the self-impaled author and of callosity for the duped publisher appeared to be another manifestation of the public's wariness of business practices in the book industry generally. In any case, the publisher came off with some scars, both internal and external, that were not deserved.

Regardless of press and public reactions, experienced publishers know that they have to trust their authors to keep them clear of egregious plagiarisms, hoaxes, or frauds. They know that they cannot possibly police the content of every manuscript that is accepted. So they have to take their risks routinely and must accept penalties philosophically when they are incurred. Indeed, wise publishers will expect occasional injury by careless or scheming authors. In time, publishers may even come to believe that chance and fate are playing games with them. Who at McGraw-Hill in 1970 would have believed that when the company moved into its new skyscraper in 1972, the name of the bank that leased the first floor facing the Avenue of the Americas would prominently label that side of the building as The Irving Trust Company?

6

Low-Keyed Business Enterprise

Having noted some of the occupational attractions and operating vagaries of book publishing, let us now examine some of the economic characteristics of the industry. Here certain causal relationships that were mentioned earlier will be clearly discernible.

Since the end of World War II, the industry has enjoyed slow but steady and healthy growth in sales volume. In the past decade alone, dollar sales more than doubled, increasing from approximately $2 billion in 1966 to $4.2 billion in 1976. The annualized rate of growth for the period was 7.7 percent. But these high-flying figures do not give a true picture, for the rate of *real* growth in constant dollars was far lower. By applying the proper dollar-price inflation factor, one discovers that the real growth in the decade was from $2 billion to $2.4 billion, and the annualized rate was only 1.8 percent. (The factor here applied is 5.774 percent per year, which is the official U.S. consumer price inflation rate for the period.) To put it another way, of the total increase in current dollar sales, only 22 percent of it was real growth in productivity, while 78 percent was the result of price inflation. How deflating is the inflation factor!

Of total sales in recent years, about 35 percent was of educational books (textbooks, manuals, workbooks, etc.) and 65 percent of other kinds of books. There are no reliable statistics on the end use of books purchased annually in the United States, but industry analysts estimate roughly that the division is about equal between educational and noneducational uses.

Many people outside publishing circles are surprised to learn that sales of general ("adult trade") and paperback books are not major portions of the industry's total sales. In the past decade, the annual sales of each of the two categories has constituted no more than 10 percent of the total dollar volume. Together they make only the tip of the iceberg that is visible to the public. And, unfortunately, they contribute less than 5 percent of the industry's annual profit. Yet, naturally enough, that visible part of the iceberg monopolizes the public attention, including that of reviewers, reporters, columnists, and commentators. That is why so many of the occasional journalistic reports on the state of the industry are so imbalanced and unreliable.

As to the industry's overall profitability, this can only be estimated from what is known of the profitability of its various segments and of the weight of each segment in the total sales composite. By that procedure, an estimate of 5–6 percent after-tax profit on sales would be approximately accurate for recent years. This rate is about average for the communications industry, but it is low by comparison with many other major U.S. industries. For other segments of the communications industry, the approximate rates in the years 1970–1975 were: newspapers, 10–11%; business magazines, 7–8%; broadcasting, 6–8%; consumer magazines, 3–4%.[1] For certain other major industries, the rates were: utilities, 12–13%; computers and office equipment, 10–11%; petroleum, 8–10%; chemicals, 7–8%; paper, 6–8%; coal, 10–12%; drugs, 10–11%.

The range of profitability among the several major segments of the book industry is quite wide. Currently, professional book publishing (scientific, technical, business, law, and medicine) is at the top with an after-tax rate on sales of 8–9%, while trade book publishing and mass-market paperback publishing are at the bottom with rates of 4–5%. The school textbook segment and the book clubs/mail-order segment each ranks near the average level with rates of 5–6%. College textbook publishing averages a little better with a rate of 6–7%.[2] On the whole, educational publishing fares far better than noneducational publishing, accounting for approximately 70% of the industry's profits on about 35% of its total sales. However, educational publishing requires larger amounts of working capital and considerably longer terms of investment—a balancing factor of some consequence.

As for rates of return on invested capital, dependable industry information is very scarce. This is because many firms are wary of revealing their balance-sheet figures—and indeed many of them, being operating units of conglomerates, do not have balance sheets of their own. However, anyone who knows about financial relationships in the major segments of the industry (such as the relationships of current assets, largely inventories and accounts receivable, to net sales and operating profits) can construct economic models indicating that the current rate of return on investment for the average profitable firm is within the range of 14–18 percent. Of course, this more attractive profit relationship is made possible by the fact that book publishers generally have very small investments, if any, in production plant and equipment.

As for capital requirements, one close student of the economic development of the book industry has estimated that in order to grow as it did in the 1960s, the industry required an input of new capital of at least $2 billion.[3] Considering their low rates of earnings, publishers certainly were not capable of plowing back anything like that much of cash profits in those years. Indeed, many firms were growing so fast that they were unable to generate any cash profits at all. How, then, was this heavy financing requirement met? By classical methods, in most cases: Companies either went public, or they merged, or they were acquired by conglomerate corporations (holding companies) that could readily supply the required investment capital. In several cases, including Dell, McGraw-Hill, Meredith, and Time-Life, cash profits on magazine publishing were used to finance rapidly expanding book publishing divisions.

No matter how the new capital was come by, it usually would increase the financial burden of the operating company. Working capital often had to be borrowed at soaring rates of interest, and cash profits were required for dividends by the parent (holding) company. Either, and sometimes both, of these requirements often depressed sustainable growth rate. This is one reason why prices of the common stocks of most publishing corporations hit the skids in the early 1970s.

As noted earlier, there are several reasons why book publishing is a low-profit industry, some obvious, others subtle and hard to perceive. Some spring from the very nature of the business; others from harmful, almost idiocratic, trade practices that are self-inflicted. The latter kind imposed upon the former has produced a generally unhealthful business climate. There is room here for no more than a sketching of the principal causes of the endemic economic weakness of the industry generally.

First, it is a relatively small and highly fractionated industry. Although, as seen, book sales have grown steadily through the years, the total annual volume remains low in the comparative scale of American industries. In the past decade, the industry's sales volume has ranked far down the line, somewhere between pet foods and processed peanut products. In any good month of the recent past, the billings of Exxon or General Motors alone have equaled the annual billings of the entire book industry. And every year as many as 60 large U.S. industrial and financial corporations have had individual sales incomes each of which is larger in volume than that of the entire book industry. As these facts suggest, the giant firms of our industry are truly no more than pygmies alongside the larger firms in such industries as automotive, electrical, chemical, petroleum, transport, and the like. And the modest sales volume of the book industry is divided among a large number of publishers. Bowker's *Literary Market Place* currently lists almost 1,000 of them, and there must be at least twice that many more specialized or local publishers that are not listed in that directory.[4] This great fractionation of an industry of modest size spells two things: (1) keen competition for authors and for the reader's dollar, and (2) a large number of small houses that, while growing, must operate at a disadvantageous economy of scale. This situation probably will continue indefinitely because it still is possible to make a "shoestring" start in most areas of book publishing.

Second, the book publisher has the costly necessity of producing and marketing each year many, many new and untried products. For each new book, there is the considerable expense of a necessarily crude research-and-development effort. Neither careful design nor prudent market testing of each new product can be afforded, hence a high risk factor is often present. Unlike most other producers of consumer goods, the publisher cannot turn out each year more and more of a few market-established products from the same designs or molds of formulas. Instead, each list must be constantly renewed by undertaking new products for which the failure rate can be high. Under these conditions, salvation lies in the ability to establish a backlist of books that can be reprinted and sold at modest expense year after year—something that usually requires plenty of time, perseverance, and accrual of working capital. And even the profit-making backlist must bear the expense of periodic revision (redesign and updating) in order to hold its own in the marketplace. Naturally, this inordinate requirement for new products in markets that are both limited and uncertain (I had almost said fickle) has a depressing effect on profits. This, too, is a built-in economic debility of the industry, yet the oppressive influence of the unavoidable risk factor has never been given due and measured recognition, not even by the bankers and investment analysts who specialize in the publishing business.

Third, the industry is saddled with a very complex, irrational, and costly marketing system. It is a grievous fact that in most areas of publishing the cost of getting a book to the buyer is higher than that of producing it. Most publishers market their wares indirectly through jobbers, specialty sales agencies, exporters, and retail booksellers; and directly to libraries, institutions, and individual customers. Paradoxically, almost all firms have many too many customers. The larger ones sell to as many as 1,000 wholesalers and 15,000 "trade" (retail) accounts, and to as many individual (direct-by-mail) customers as they can find—and some manage to find as many as 100,000 to 200,000 of the latter in a good year. (Annually, the industry's direct sales to consumers just about equal the volume of sales through retailers.) Serving such a myriad of customers is not only costly, it also causes confusion and unhealthful competition in the marketplace. What the industry sorely needs is an effective system for wholesale distribution of its product, but most publishers are firmly addicted to the habit of selling directly to any customer who wants to buy. They think they have to do so because very few wholesalers have as yet offered adequate service for either the publishers or the retail book trade. More will be said about this problem in a later chapter.

The greatest flaw in the industry's marketing system is, certainly, the high cost of handling returns of unsold books. This cost has grown alarmingly in recent years and it is now the bête noir of the industry. Yet most publishers have been reluctant to face its baleful influence on profits, much less to attempt corrective measures. Almost all houses have ground rules that are supposed to limit returns, but they are more often ignored than enforced. As a result, profitless out-and-in shipments have soared to almost unbelievable levels in several major areas of publishing. The highest rate is in mass-market paperbacks where returns credits now equal about 46% of the value of net sales. Rates in other large areas are: college texts, 18%; trade books, 16%; professional books, 14%.

Publishers have, of course, long deplored these high rates of returns. (One doyen of the industry, Alfred Knopf, is said to have remarked ruefully, "It seems that much of my inventory is gone today and here tomorrow.") But the industry has made no attempt to count the cost, much less to try for possibly acceptable reforms. My private analysis indicates that the expense of the double handling of unsold books is currently about $60 million annually. This is the publishers' expense of out-and-in handling costs alone, not including carriage charges, which customarily are paid by the customers. It seems reasonable to guess that the customers who make the returns incur at least an equal amount of expense. Therefore, the total annual cost to the book trade must be well over $120 million.

Now, admittedly, it is impossible to formulate even a rough estimate of how many more books are sold by reason of the liberal return allowances. All that can be said for certain is that the present practice is almost universally accepted as being a very costly but necessary evil. Indeed, many publishers and most booksellers believe that if liberal return privileges were discontinued, the whole book distribution system would collapse overnight. However, we shall never know about this until publishers and dealers alike are willing to venture some sort of harsh remedy for which there is no money-back guarantee.

Another reason why book publishing is a low-profit industry is the slow pace of technological progress in its production methods and processes. Until very recent years, only a few publishers made even modest investments in research-and-development efforts aimed at reducing production costs, and book manufacturers did little more on their own. In the past decade, however, advances in computer-assisted composition have substantially reduced both the time and cost factors in producing several kinds of books, especially those that must be revised and republished periodically, such as almanacs, directories, handbooks, dictionaries, and encyclopedias. Further, the wide employment of vastly improved techniques of photocomposition (typesetting on film) has eliminated much of the hand-skill technology and the accompanying high cost of traditional hot-metal composition. Photocomposition has also greatly reduced the typesetting cost of books that have high content of numerical and symbolic characters. Here typesetting that was formerly done by a combination of Monotype and hand composition is now done on monofilm, which is an application of monotype equipment to photocomposition on film rather than with metal. This process has effected big savings in the composition of complex mathematical equations, chemical compounds, design and computational formulas, and other similar matter.

The introduction of photocomposition has been followed by integrated systems for the keyboarding of manuscripts on computer tapes that allow proofing and editing at video display terminals located at publishers' offices. Thus staff editors now can control the keyboarding of manuscripts and can make necessary corrections on computer disks of tapes before the copy goes to the compositor. Such systems give the publisher better control of both the cost and the quality of composition. They also speed up the production process, which always produces an indirect saving of cost as well as a direct satisfaction to authors, who are, quite naturally, impatient to see bound copies of their books.

Some significant advances have been made also in the technology of presswork and binding. Gigantic offset web presses that deliver folded sheets now produce books at rates of high speed and low cost that were undreamed of 30 to 40 years ago. One of the most notable of all improvements has come in the cost and durability of adhesive binding, which has not been as widely accepted and used as it should be.

It must be noted, however, that most of the new printing-press technology can be applied only to straight-matter books that are printed in quantities of 10,000 copies or more. This means that about 60 percent of the new books published today do not qualify (or, rather, quantify) for the larger benefits. But there has been some economic gain in the development of short-run offset web presses that deliver folded signatures and permit very fast plate changes and low spoilage of paper. These presses eliminate much of the slow and costly "make-ready" operation that is necessary in changing plates on the old-style letterpress machines.

Thus, although progress has been made in some areas of book production technology, there has been no truly revolutionary advance in several decades. And certainly the advances that have been made have not resulted in the large reductions in production costs that most other industries have enjoyed.

In addition to the economic encumbrances that have been described, there is a pervasive psychological reason why book publishing is a low-profit industry. This is the fact that far too many "accidental" publishers are not good businesspeople by either nature or inclination. Some of us are ex-editors on whom the dollar sign has not been impressed with sufficient firmness, or we are ex–sales managers who like to sell and sell and sell without proper regard for margins and expense. Others of us have been wrongly brought up in the tradition that the business side—the need to make a profit—is the responsibility of the chaps in the back office. Still others, but only a few, vocally pride themselves in their disinterest in the mundane business affairs of their firms. In any case, business ineptness, whether real or affected, is harmful to the book industry and to its public image, and especially so in the minds of bankers and investors. This public image, like the contradictive image of Scrooge, is something that should be repudiated whenever and wherever possible.

I have a friend, a solid and successful leader of our industry, who was once introduced to an audience of his peers and lessers: "Ladies and gentlemen, I now give you Horace Hardbound, who is not only a great publisher but a good businessman as well." My friend Horace (anonymous, of course) seized the opportunity to reject the double label, protesting strongly that it was a senseless redundancy, that every good publisher is perforce a good businessperson. The sharpness of his retort appeared to discomfit some members of his audience who apparently preferred to think of book publishing as a high-minded intellectual pursuit, not a grubbing commercial occupation.

7

Twin Evils: Underpricing and Overprinting

Next to the editorial selection and perfection of worthy manuscripts, the publisher's most important functions lie on the business side of the enterprise. They are the exercise of rigid pricing and close inventory control, both of which are highly essential to profitability. But both are operating nettles of the prickliest sort, and woe betide the publisher who does not grasp them firmly. For what does it profit the house to sell a carload of an excellent book if the price is too low to yield a minimal margin? Or what does it profit to sell a carload at the right price if, in the end, the cost of unsold inventory wipes out most of the margin on the books that have been sold?

As consumer products go, books have always been peculiarly difficult to price effectually. Each book must stand more or less on its own in its marketplace, and usually there is no established norm for competitive pricing. Moreover, in pricing most new books, the anticipated volume of sale is as important as the base manufacturing cost. To these economic complications must be added an equally difficult human factor, because the author, the editor, and even the sales manager usually want every book priced at the lowest possible figure. (Lower prices sell more books, they argue; and, besides, one must think of the poor student and the impecunious lay reader.) Thus, solving the economic riddle and mitigating the often clamorous human factor are dual problems that must be dealt with firmly when each new book is priced. And the ever-present risk factor must also be considered. Even if it does seem greedy, the sure-fire best-sellers should always be overpriced in order to compensate for the unknown but sure-fire losers that lurk in every season's list. Young editors and salespeople generally find it hard to understand and accept these imperatives of sound pricing policy.

Only in recent years has the book industry recovered from its underpricing folly that followed World War II. Both costs and prices had been frozen through the war period, but when the restrictions were lifted, printers and binders were quick to make up for lost time. Book production costs soared—by more than 80 percent within two years. Yet, strangely enough, there was at the same time a great emotional urge in the book trade to keep prices down to prewar levels—an urge that was shared by most booksellers and many idealistic publishers. This economically wacky notion was taken up and promoted vigorously by—of all people—the editors of *Publishers Weekly*. Week after week, *PW* editorialized on the subject at a crusading pitch, and a good number of well-known publishers joined the crusade. Indeed, a dozen or so firms went overboard and announced that they were reducing prices in order to give their books a deserved advantage over other kinds of consumer goods. Each was given an editorial "gold star" by *PW*, and all were applauded by prominent booksellers around the country. (This at a time when booksellers needed, more than anything else, larger dollar margins to take care of their rapidly mounting overhead expense.) It was truly a time of economic madness in the industry, and it lasted, unfortunately, for several years. As late as 1949, *PW* was able to report with satisfaction that book prices had increased since 1939 by only 35 percent while the general cost-of-living index had risen by 74.2 percent. More than a year later *PW* observed editorially:

Book publishing is certainly not in a favorable position for another round of cost increases. Most producers, from barbers to builders, have been able (and willing) in recent years to raise prices to consumers as their own costs were increased. The producers of books have not been able to do much in the way of following that practice. There has been a justified feeling that books can be easily priced out of their market.[1]

Looking back on the naïvety of that untimely, industry-wide urge for low prices, one can only wonder how many millions in profits it cost publishers and booksellers in the two decades following the war. Even when publishers began to realize the folly of it, their price base was then so low that it took another decade to bring it up to a satisfactory level.

To me, at the time an unseasoned publishing executive, this pressure for holding prices down while costs were soaring was most perplexing. Indeed, I was astounded that it was so widely accepted. And I was distressed to observe that most of my editorial and sales colleagues at McGraw-Hill warmly supported the *PW* position. That made my job—my duty—much more difficult. For I was convinced that book prices had to go up and go up fast, else the industry would soon be in trouble. This conviction had been bred into me, I suppose, because years before, in a family hardware business down in Kentucky, my father had taught me the importance of price maintenance. I could clearly recall his customary banter with such a man as the farmer who always wanted to buy at a cut rate:

"Now see here, Mr. Benjamin, I'm an old friend. Seems like you ought to knock a dollar off the price of this horse collar."

"Yes sir, it does seem that way, my friend, but you've got to remember two things. First, I must make my living off my friends because my enemies never come into my store. Second, I've got to make a profit on the goods I sell because this place is full of stuff that nobody seems to want to buy at any price."

Usually this kind of exchange would produce a laugh and a sale at the price marked on the merchandise. And my father would always grumble, when the customer had left, that he did not so much mind losing money on goods that he didn't sell, but he'd be hanged before he'd take a loss on what he *did* sell. Further, my father believed that inventory should always be priced at replacement cost, not at actual cost—and twice a year he would mark up all the larger inventory items in accordance with the latest costs quoted by the jobbers from whom he customarily bought.

Is it not strange that such a simple and sensible pricing strategy was so well known to a small-town merchant in the hills of Kentucky, yet so foreign to the business thinking of many leading book publishers in New York and other metropolitan centers? That the soundness of it did escape many publishers was one of the reasons (along with looming inheritance taxes) why a number of privately owned publishing houses, operating mostly with owned capital, ran short in the 1950s and 1960s and had to merge or "go public." It was also the main reason why so many old-line British houses found themselves in financial trouble in the same period.

Yet the industry's reluctance to raise prices did not end with the 1960s. As late as 1977, a leading publisher of "literary" books, Roger W. Straus, Jr., would remark ruefully: "The trouble with hardcover books is that none of us raised our prices soon enough when our costs started to hit the ceiling. It's true throughout the industry—no one had the nerve to raise prices adequately. We finally put them up three years ago. . . ."[2]

As for the second key to profitability—tight control of inventory—I soon learned that this is best done by the publisher as a strictly centralized function in a house with a large and diversified list. Far from being routine, it is actually a complex, sensitive, and hence a difficult function. Certainly, it cannot be turned over to someone "on the business side," nor can it be trusted to an editor or a sales manager. The "business side" knows too little about the product and its market. The editor too often has a bad case of "author fever," which comes from sharing the author's excitement at the prospect of large and immediate sales. The sales manager also often has a touch of author fever, and in any case is usually by nature an optimistic and expansive person. And, as noted earlier, editors and sales managers both like to see large printings that will bring down unit costs and prices. Both are inclined to push for overly large first printings—the surest road to ruin in the book business. So it is left to the top publishing executive—the orchestra leader—to decide in a cool, detached, calculated way just how many copies of each new book shall be printed for inventory.

Beginning publishers soon learn that they, too, can often catch author fever, either directly or from infection via the editor. It is altogether too easy to reach hopefully for a fat profit margin by yielding to pleas for larger printings. Then, there is often the risk that a book will take off in high gear immediately on publication and go out of stock before a second printing can be provided. Oh, the shame of it! And the bitter recriminations that always follow—the ire of the sales manager, the hurt looks of the editor, and the scalding letters from the outraged and ruined author! Every time this happens, the publisher suffers a proper amount of humiliation and inwardly promises not to be so conservative the next time. Yet there are always evident some painful examples of overprintings and unsalable stocks, about which little is said by members of the staff. Nevertheless, the wise publisher has a strict policy of no recrimination for failures. Editors must not be upbraided for their mistakes of judgment, else they will too quickly hesitate to take the reasonable risks that are inherent in the book business. No, absolutely no recrimination—but if editors make too many mistakes in overestimating markets, they will in time be invited to look for other jobs.

In order to understand the insidious temptation to reach for lower unit costs by increasing the size of first printings, one has to understand the economy of scale in book production. This is a very simple calculus of cost factors that is not well enough understood by many people in the book industry and by most people on its fringes.

In accounting for production costs, the customary division is between "fixed" costs and "variable" costs. The former are the costs that go for the making of the theoretical first copy. It is the same amount, no matter whether 1,000 or 100,000 copies are to be printed. In arriving at a "unit" (or per-copy) cost, the amount of the fixed costs must, of course, be spread over the quantity of the first printing. Thus it is highly important in long-run printings.

The elements of fixed costs are (1) the expense of editing, design, and proofreading; and (2) the so-called "plant" costs of composition (typesetting), artwork for illustrations, photo plate preparation, and a few minor items. The variable costs are the

ECONOMY OF SCALE IN BOOK PRODUCTION

		Number of Copies (Thousands)						
		1.0	2.5	5	10	25	50	100
FIXED COSTS								
Editing, design, proofing	$ 1,900							
Plant Costs:								
Composition	5,600							
Artwork for illustrations	800							
Photo plate preparation	1,500							
Miscellaneous	200							
Total fixed costs	$10,000	$10.00	$4.00	$2.00	$1.00	$0.40	$0.20	$0.10
VARIABLE COSTS								
Printing		.41	.20	.13	.09	.09	.09	.08
Paper		.27	.25	.25	.24	.24	.24	.24
Binding (hardcover sewn)		.62	.50	.46	.44	.42	.37	.35
Subtotal		$1.30	$ .95	$ .84	$ .77	$ .75	$ .70	$ .67
TOTAL PER COPY COST		$11.30	$4.95	$2.84	$1.77	$1.15	$ .90	$ .77

48

three components of "manufacturing" costs, namely, paper, presswork, and binding. Of these, only the cost of presswork varies importantly with the quantity of copies printed. The per-copy cost of paper and binding is almost the same no matter how large the print order is beyond the first few thousand copies.

By putting all the production cost components together in a tabulation that shows the effect of both the fixed and the variable costs in a wide range of printing quantities, one can easily perceive how the economy of scale affects the per-copy cost. The accompanying table is based on 1976 costs of producing a typical 324-page book in a 6-by-9-inch format with Smyth-sewn sheets and hardcover binding.

This model tabulation dramatizes the high cost of small printings; it also discloses how quickly the law of diminishing returns set in with respect to the reduction of per-copy cost by increasing the size of printings. This phenomenon explains the sore temptation to increase short printings of specialized books. It also explains why increasing the size of long-run printings has so little economic attraction. It is, in fact, the main reason why first printings are prudently kept down in size to a level that is surprising to most people who are not familiar with the economics of book production. For example, at McGraw-Hill—a large firm with a widely varying list of over 400 new hardbound titles each year—the average first printing is currently about 9,000 copies, while the median size is about 5,000 copies.

If presiding over the birth of a book is difficult, presiding over its death and burial is just as difficult and even more painful. And the burial of a failure, of a book that never got off the ground, is an especially painful event. Into the grave of such a book go countless hours of the author's work and a large chunk of his ambition and hope, plus a measure of frustration of the sales staff, plus a quantum of the house's prestige and amour-propre. Then there is, of course, the material matter of the overstock—several hundred or several thousand copies—that must be ground up for pulp or sold at a paltry price to a dealer in book "remainders." Yet in each case someone must decide, coldly and objectively, the precise time when a book must be declared a failure, when the author's disappointment must be swallowed, when the company must take its loss on the unsold inventory.

That someone is, of course, the publisher, the orchestra leader. And usually a negative decision is conditioned by lingering hopes that somehow new life can be breathed into a moribund title. But the experienced publisher knows that the cost of carrying dead inventory is very high, that failures must be recognized and liquidated promptly if accretions of loss are to be avoided. And, in doing the necessary, he sadly perceives that the lot of a policeman of book inventory is not a happy one.

8

The Mystique
of Marketing

The problem of inventory control would not be so difficult, certainly, if publishers were able to develop scientific techniques of book marketing—if they could predict market demands and preferences with a reasonable degree of certainty. This they have never been able to do. Hence, except in the areas of textbooks and of professional and reference book publishing, the marketing of books has remained an art—and almost a "black" art, at that. Even the most seasoned publisher has to admit that very little is known about why the general public will prefer one author over another or one book over all others of its kind. So in marketing, the publisher often can do no better than follow topical or faddist or fashionable trends of public interest. And, while high literary standards may be insisted upon, it is clear that in the real world of books one cannot depend on quality to translate into popularity, this because one sees, year in and year out, immediate demand and large sales of second- and third-rate books. In the end, it becomes obvious that public taste and preference can be not only uncertain and unpredictable but debased and fickle as well.

Given this view of the marketplace for general-interest books, it is not surprising that publishers are skeptical of the value of extensive market research, even if the cost could be afforded for individual titles. Rightly or wrongly, they see themselves forced to gauge new-book markets by relevant past experience with similar books and by intuitive guesses of when the public appetite for a faddish or modish kind of book has been whetted and when satiated.

Since publishers have such unsure knowledge of the public interest and taste in reading matter, it follows that they would have little faith in the effectiveness of consumer advertising of books. Accordingly, the industry is ruled by the traditional wisdom that advertising will increase the sale of a book that the public has taken to, but it will not sell a book that has not somehow made a start under its own power. Burdened with this kind of wisdom, most publishers budget advertising expense for each new book quite strictly and watch the results very carefully. The usual rule-of-thumb practice is to budget for each new title a set percentage of the value of estimated sales for the first year. If early sales exceed the estimate, added advertising dollars will be spent; if sales do not come up to expectations, the budgeted amount may not be spent. This is, to be sure, rather a conservative and mechanical procedure, and certainly it is something that many authors are troubled to understand. Nevertheless, most publishers do stick quite rigidly to a budgetary formula, even though they often are embattled by disappointed authors who are sure that more advertising would produce more sales. The issue is a classical example of built-in conflict of interest: The publisher is sure that additional sales, if any, will be made at a loss, while the author knows that royalty must be paid, even if the selling cost does wipe out the publisher's margin for profit. Small wonder that this issue can quickly sour the onsetting sweetness of many author-publisher partnership relations.

Although publishers generally are dubious of the value of consumer advertising, they do have confidence in the power of other, and less costly, kinds of book promotion. Accordingly, they are usually quite generous with expense for review copies, for publicity through the press, for exposure of authors at bookstores and on radio and TV programs, and for advertising to the trade, meaning the sellers of books, both wholesalers and retailers.

It is generally recognized that for certain kinds of books, and especially for those addressed to professional readers or critical general readers, press reviews are very important—that their influence will often make or break a book's chance of success. On the other hand, unfavorable reviews of "trashy" books seem not to hurt at all—the uncritical general reader will buy with total disregard of the reviewers' critical dicta. Clearly, casual book buyers may not know much about literature, but they do know what they like to read. All successful publishers and their advertising agents learn, in time, to live with this bald fact.

The effectiveness of author exposure as a promotional device depends, naturally, on the particular author's personal charisma and articulateness before an audience—plus the book's appeal to the general public. Here again, publishers often are dubious of the direct effectiveness of this kind of promotion, but they are keenly aware of its important side effect on the happiness of the involved authors and their agents, and this alone can be worth the effort and expense incurred.

Since the casual reader of general books—the reader who is motivated largely by word-of-mouth recommendations, or by best-seller lists, or by the popularity of "talked-about" titles and authors—is hard to reach and influence, almost all publishers concentrate their promotion on sales to the relatively small hard core of habitual book buyers. These are the regular customers of bookstores and the readers of newspapers and magazines that consistently carry notices and reviews and advertisements of new books. The exemplar of these hard-core customers is the constant reader of the *New York Times Book Review* or other similar publications. Therefore, publishers concentrate their advertising in such publications, and it is there that publicity handouts most often appear in print. Indeed, it is no secret that publishers advertise in them for several purposes, some overt and some covert. Though an advertisement in the *New York Times Book Review* is ostensibly directed to book buyers, it actually is as much intended to influence booksellers. It is intended also to attract the notice of book reviewers and editors of the book pages of other newspapers and magazines. Further, it may well engage the attention of directors of book clubs and of people who are interested in buying reprint, cinema, dramatization, or translation rights. Finally, as indicated earlier, it will be sure to please the author and the agent, and it may even serve to attract other authors and agents to the house that is known to advertise its wares. Yes, the advantages of such advertising are both multiple and patent; still it must be confessed that even the most experienced and astute publisher does not know how well "it pays to advertise" in the traditional media.

The publishers' uncertainty about the value of traditional book advertising has carried over strongly to their exploration of TV and radio as media for reaching mass markets. Since only a small fraction of the new books published annually have mass-market appeal, and since the cost of a major TV campaign is at least $100,000, only a few publishers have been adventurous enough to give it a serious try, even with their best-sellers. There are several basic reasons why most publishers have hesitated to plunge into such deep water.

First, they know that habitual book buyers are a very thin cross section of the general population, hence there are not enough ready customers in the TV audience to justify the relatively large expense of TV campaigns. There is no point, they reason, in spending that amount of money on reaching many people who are not book buyers and only a few who are. They are not encouraged by a recent survey that indicated that only 25 percent of the total U.S. population, including students, bought at least one book, hardcover or paperback, in the six-month period preceding the survey.

Second, they believe that their profit margins are too narrow to permit such costly advertising in such thin markets.

Third, they are convinced that retail distribution is not wide enough to back up mass-market advertising except for the few best-sellers that are likely to be stocked at supermarkets, drug and variety stores, railroad stations, airline terminals, and similar outlets. (There are no more than ten or eleven thousand outlets for hardcover books in the entire United States.)

In spite of the generally recognized hazards, a few publishers have jumped, experimentally and up to knee-deep, into TV advertising—and with encouraging degrees of success in most instances. As might be expected, they have been more successful with paperbacks than with hardcover titles. Indeed, their experience suggests that it is difficult to persuade price-conscious mass-market purchasers to pay $10 or $15 for a new and popular hardcover title when they know that they can wait a year or so and buy it for one-fifth of that price.

In any case, it appears that books having prominent news value or topicality are the most likely to succeed in TV campaigns. And, naturally, such books have a chance of success in their hardcover editions—interested readers do not want to wait for the cheaper paperback reprints. The same goes for sensational novels and biographies, for exposés of any kind, and for books written by celebrities of all stripes. The experts say that for such books TV advertising can successfully appeal to the audience's desire to know what the excitement is all about *now*. And, not surprisingly, they say also that such books having a special appeal to women are the most likely to succeed.

Another category that has been successfully promoted by TV (and radio as well) is the do-it-yourself books, with a range in subjects all the way from home repairs and vegetable gardening to weight-watching, transcendental meditation, and getting more out of your sex life after 50.

Obviously, publishers still have a lot to learn about the cost/benefit of TV advertising. It appears that, under present conditions, the medium can be applied successfully to only a small fraction of the new books published annually. Yet there is reason to hope that eventually TV promotion may show the way to the building of a larger market base for general books, something our industry sorely needs.

In very recent years, the marketing efforts of certain publishers have been greatly assisted by the modernized merchandising methods of a few wholesale distributors and of several large chains of retail bookstores. By supplying publishers and retail outlets with computer-based information on sales and inventories of selected lists of books that the public is buying heavily, these large-scale merchandisers help the publishers to gauge and control their inventories of fast-selling titles. The computerized reporting systems tell the publishers what books are selling where and in what quantities, and of course the data helps both publishers and booksellers to anticipate both buildups and slowdowns in demand. Naturally, this kind of information also helps retailers to maximize inventory turnover and to minimize out-of-stock situations. It also helps both publishers and booksellers to reduce the risk of being caught with serious amounts of overstocks.

One of the largest of the computer-based sales and inventory information systems is operated by the Chas. Levy Circulating Company of Chicago, a wholesale distributor of books to some 3,500 mass-market retailers. Called "The Book Merchandising & Information System," it documents sales and returns of each of its retail customers for over 6,000 paperback titles and about 500 basic hardcover titles of which the company carries large wholesale stocks. The system reports retail sales demographically; compares sales with returns, title by title; compares sales by categories of books (mysteries, gothics, science fiction, humor, politics, sex, etc.); and even compares customer-preferred authors within categories. Promoting the system to retail booksellers, its proprietor boasts: "We can spot the beginning or end of sales trends faster than ever before to enable you to jump on or off the bandwagon according to your customers' buying preferences." It is also claimed that the systems assistance to inventory control has reduced the rate of returns of unsold books by about one-third of the average for the industry—a great boon, certainly, for the more than 50 publishers that this distributor represents.

Similar, but less sophisticated, merchandising information systems are operated by the country's largest two retail bookstore chains, B. Dalton and Waldenbooks. And similar kinds of sales reporting and inventory control systems are now employed by several of the very large chains of general retail stores that have recently started to exploit mass markets for books in a big way, including Wards, Sears Roebuck, and J. C. Penney.[1]

Naturally, all publishers of mass-market books view the advent of these modern merchandising systems with a great deal of excitement. For the first time, retail bookselling has been given a departure from the occupational elegancy that it has suffered for many, many decades. But it must be remembered that, innovative as they may be, the merchandising techniques involved can be applied to only a small fraction of the new titles and reprints that are published each year and to no more than an infinitesimal fraction of the publishers' backlist titles that continue to sell steadily year after year. Furthermore, these techniques can be applied, obviously, to only those titles and authors that have established themselves as very popular current favorites with the general public. Lamentably, they are of little help in meeting the publishers' desperate need for prepublication market research of a kind that can be afforded for run-of-the-mill titles. While they do provide some valuable insights of market behavior for certain categories of books generally, they are, alas, of but little value in predicting sales of individual titles that have not been published.

Nevertheless, the book industry as a whole can rejoice that a merchandising breakthrough has been scored in the 1960s and the 1970s. Now we can reasonably hope that ways will be found to bring book marketing into the twentieth century before it comes to the end.

9

Neglect of Product Promotion

Strangely, the book industry's narcissistic propensity to exalt itself and its product has caused it to neglect its own interest in an important kind of generalized promotional activity. This is the need to promote books as a highly desirable class of consumer goods. Many publishers—and especially publishers of belletristic books—seem to think that their books are so good and so much to be desired that the public should feel privileged to be able to come and get them. Indeed, some publishers appear to think it a shame that their precious wares have to be vended like other consumer products. They disdain even a scintilla of huckstering. All this is why the book industry generally has done next to nothing in the way of general production promotion, why it has spent so little of its time or resources on convincing the public that books are indeed as valuable and rewarding as they, the publishers, think they are. And this is perhaps a good part of the reason why the American public spends such an infinitesimal part of its disposable income for the purchase of books.

If book publishers would look around the business world at what other industries spend on product promotion, they would see many striking contrasts with their own view of the matter. For example, the TV broadcasting industry, whose annual sales income is about the same as that of the book industry, spends over $1.6 million annually on selling the general value of TV as an advertising medium. And the Tea Council of the United States of America spends $1 million per year on promoting the pleasures of drinking tea, of which the annual wholesale cost is about $200 million. And sugar wholesalers spend about the same amount on keeping the United States sweet on sugar, of which the sales value is something like $2.5 billion annually. And cotton cloth manufacturers, with a wholesale income of about $2.8 billion, spend about $5 million annually promoting the general advantages of buying cotton goods. (What is more, the cotton cloth industry is clever enough to get the Federal government to contribute about three-fifths of its product promotion budget each year.) Yet the book industry trade associations—with the notable exception of the Children's Book Council—which by their own lights have the greatest product in the world, never spent more than $100,000 in any one year on general product promotion up to 1976—and most of this paltry expense was shelled out cautiously by college publishers in their efforts to convince students and teachers that textbooks have more than transient value and hence should not be sold to used-book dealers for a pittance when courses are finished.

Now, how can the exceptional attitude of the publishers of children's books be accounted for? Well, it started with the idea of Children's Book Week, originated by Franklin K. Mathiews of the Boy Scouts of America, and was first organized in 1919 by booksellers and librarians under the leadership of Frederic G. Melcher, who had just become managing editor of *Publishers Weekly*. It was administered for some years by the National Association of Book Publishers, and from 1934 to 1945 by the Bowker office, with its program expanding greatly. At that point, the newly formed Association of Children's Book Editors set up the Children's Book Council as a year-round center to handle Book Week and other activities. Using members' dues as well as income from the sale of Book Week promotion pieces, the council has aggressively developed effective programs and materials to promote childrens' books among librarians, teachers, booksellers, and parents.

In addition to its Book Week, the council now has a year-round promotional effort directed each year to a particular genre of children's books—for example, children's poetry, children's pets, children's sports, etc. It also produces continually renewed materials for sponsored summer reading programs, and it is responsible for several published lists of the best of children's books produced annually in different categories of specialized interest. On the whole, its program is imaginative, yet practical, and forward looking. In recent years, its budget has been just under a half-million dollars.[1]

Considering the industry's broad indifference to product promotion, many observers were surprised by the announcement, at midyear 1976, that the General Book Division of the AAP had provided $150,000 for TV promotion of the theme "A Book Is a Loving Gift." The resulting commercials were run in two pilot metropolitan areas, New York and Minneapolis, at the end of the year. The results were encouraging enough to convince the General Book Division that the public's awareness of books as approbative gifts can be enough influenced by institutional advertising to create extra sales in substantial amounts, especially in the pre-Christmas season. Accordingly, that division committed itself to raise $400,000 ($300,000 within the book industry and $100,000 from outside sources) to continue the experiment at the end of 1977 in eight or ten of the best book-buying metropolitan areas of the country. Naturally, all publishers and booksellers are watching this daring (for the book industry) and encouraging promotional experiment with much interest.

Another stirring of interest in institutional promotion came early in 1977, when the School Book Division of the AAP announced a program aimed at winning a greater share of the educational dollar for textbooks and other instructional materials. This program, scheduled in two phases over an 18-month period, was budgeted at $100,000. It was described to a *Publishers Weekly* reporter as follows:

> The major new program announced at this year's meeting was an attack on the problem of shrinking educational spending on materi-

als, now less than 1% of all educational funds. To try to regain this ground and win more, the school division has engaged Barry Conforte and his firm, Motivational Communications, to generate an intensive public relations campaign aimed at school administrators, board members and parents in local communities to educate them as to the value and cost/effectiveness of better materials in achieving better education for their children. A national campaign to raise general awareness will be conducted through placement of articles and speakers in strategic media and programs, as well as the creation of newsletters and other promotional literature. At the same time, a pilot district program will be aimed at three carefully chosen school districts to try to shift their attitudes and perceptions at the local level. . . . In the second phase, the most successful techniques from the pilot district campaign will be incorporated into the national campaign, which will be expanded and intensified.[2]

Can these two exploratory new programs be taken as auguries of a slow awakening of publishers generally to the values of institutionalized product promotion? Let us devoutly hope so, for this kind of action is long, long overdue.

A good case study of its idiosyncratic behavior could be made of the failure of the book industry to support the book promotional programs of the National Book Committee. To my way of thinking, this failure was the most puzzling instance of business nonfeasance in the history of American publishing. And it was, surely, a sad reflection of the industry's inability to carry on a national group activity that required sustained cooperation and common confidence and respect among its members. This is, to be sure, a harsh judgment, but no harsher than was the industry's neglect and final abandonment of the committee, which was its own creation and largely its own creature.

The National Book Committee was organized in 1954. It was started as a national organization of 100 people of some national prominence who were willing to help promote the societal value of books. The concept was first proposed by two of the most highly respected publishers of the period, Cass Canfield and Harold Guinzburg. They persuaded the governing board of the ABPC (American Book Publishers Council) that the trade association should serve as organizing agent for the committee, and thereafter the organizational effort was very ably programmed and managed by Dan Lacy, then executive director of the ABPC.

By design—and for the sake of a proper balancing of interests—only a few book publishers were included in the membership. Naturally, this peeved a good many others who thought they should have been included. Strike one against the committee and its organizers.

The National Book Committee initially undertook two major promotional programs, National Library Week and National Book Awards. The former was jointly sponsored by the ABPC and the ALA (American Library Association), the latter by the ABPC, the ABA (American Booksellers Association), and the NACS (National Association of College Stores). The former had to struggle from the start to establish a proper format for credibility and prestige; the latter was highly successful on a national scale from the beginning.

The National Book Awards, started in 1960, suffered continual dissatisfaction, dissension, and hard knocks. To those of us who tried for many years to make the program measure up to its purpose and promise, it seemed that no one, not even the winners of the awards, would ever be happy with it. Authors, publishers, booksellers, and critics alike constantly quarreled over questions of selected categories for awards, selection of judges, nominations of candidates, criteria for judging, secrecy of decisions, and the programming of the annual awards ceremony itself.

Some of the disagreement was justified, for the program truly was ineptly managed in certain years. But much of it was no more than supercilious carping, usually motivated by jealousy, pique, or haughty intellectual prejudice. In spite of the constant dissatisfaction, the National Book Awards survived and prospered slowly but surely. In time, the annual affair would enjoy nationwide publicity, which in many instances would add no more than a modicum to the sale of the prize-winning selection. Still, the public's awareness of the world of books was undeniably increased year after year in a beneficial way.

The National Library Week, started in 1958, was, as noted earlier, an altogether different story. The promotional materials and the operational strategy for each year's event were planned by a guiding subcommittee of the National Book Committee, but most of the work was done by thousands of librarians and local volunteers throughout the country. No questioning or bickering or carping here; obviously, librarians know what is good for them and their profession. Also, unlike book publishers, they knew how to pull together very effectively. What is more, the librarians or their institutions gladly paid the cost of the promotional materials created by the National Book Committee staff. From the beginning, their success at propagandizing the values of libraries, books, and lifetime reading habits was truly prodigious. Indeed, they were so successful that National Library Week was widely credited with the generation of grass-roots pressures that changed public policy on Federal support of non-Federal libraries. In the 1960s, under the Kennedy and Johnson administrations, that support was increased from $2.3 million to approximately $200 million annually—and concurrently the purchase of books by libraries was increased fourfold. Later, the same grass-roots pressures would encourage the Congress to override three of Nixon's regressive vetoes of education and library assistance acts, and this boosted book sales by many millions in the early 1970s.

In addition to the two major programs just described, the National Book Committee awarded the annual National Medal for Literature (a $5,000 prize provided by the Harold Guinzburg Fund), and annually organized several conferences on the promotion of books and reading. Also, it sponsored the publication of a number of books of the same promotional character, including Nancy Larrick's *A Parent's Guide to Children's Reading* and *The Freedom to Read* by Richard McKeon, Robert Merton, and Walter Gellhorn. The former, currently in its third edition, has sold more than one million copies.

Now, one would suppose that all this propagandism would have been quite costly. Not so at all. In fact, the annual operating budget of the National Book Committee at its largest was slightly over $400,000, and about 50 percent of this amount was earned each year by the sale of National Library Week materials. Book publishers contributed only 18 percent of the total, a proportion that usually was matched by other donors, private and corporate. Beyond its cash contributions, the book industry—through the AAP—contributed staff assistance that was valued at about seventy to eighty thousand dollars annually. It is hard to imagine a better cost/benefit bargain for the U.S. book trade as a whole.

Yet, in 1974, pleading a financial crunch, the book industry withdrew its support and let the National Book Committee go down the drain. This default came after twenty years of struggle for adequate backing of the efforts of scores of public-spirited citizens who had spent untold days and nights working selflessly for the objectives of the committee. They could hardly believe that the book industry would be so niggardly and so neglectful of its own interests. To most of them it was a sad betrayal, but some of them were not too much surprised. They had seen how much publishers love to quarrel among themselves, especially when dissent provides an excuse to keep the purse strings tight.

Fortunately, the extinction of the National Book Committee did not result in the abandonment of its major programs. The ALA has since carried on National Library Week with little loss of momentum. And a dedicated member of the defunct committee, Roger L. Stevens, personally assumed responsibility for the National Book Awards and the National Medal for Literature presentations. (He was the committee's last chairman.) With his own private funds and other substantial donations by a few large corporations (mostly nonpublishing), he managed to carry on with a minimum of book industry involvement—for which he probably was thankful. After that, the awards were sponsored for two years by the prestigious National Academy/Institute of Arts and Letters. But the continued squabbling among publishers and authors and critics soon became too much for the august academicians; they quietly turned the sponsorship over to the AAP in the summer of 1977. (Financing will be provided mainly by The Franklin Library, which in turn is financed by The Franklin Mint.) Considering the implications of this direct involvement of the book publishers' trade association, it seems likely that the squabbling will soon rise to an unbearable volume and pitch of discordance.

At this point, the reader is entitled to ask why the deplorable history of the defunct National Book Committee should now be rehashed. My recording of it has three purposes, all of them quite obvious: first, to demonstrate the book industry's traditional blindness to the value of general product promotion; second, to show how shamelessly publishers will sit on their hands while others work in their behalf; third, to record a past instance of senseless group behavior in the hope that new and younger people in the industry will see the need to change its mind-set on the matter.

For my part, I often have thought that this neglect syndrome, this psychologically based failure of book publishers to support their own sterling products in the marketplace, is something that should long ago have had the attention of an industrial psychiatrist.

10

Too Many Books?

American book publishers generally suffer another syndrome that would make an interesting study by industrial psychiatrists. This is their unfortunate apprehension of increased size or of bigness in almost any form. This pervasive phobia has its most pronounced manifestation in the often-expressed belief that many too many books are being published. Hardly a month goes by without a blast of public complaint by a publisher or a book reviewer or a librarian or some other observer on the fringes of the business. It is very familiar wailing, heard year after year, and it usually is accompanied by the claim that senseless overproduction is rapidly ruining the book business.

It has been noted that book publishing is shot through with vagaries and paradoxes. None of them is more puzzling to me than the industry's disdain of its own success in the marketplace. Why is it that, as more and more publishers each year set higher and higher records of new-book production and sales, the wailing grows louder and louder? The answer, I think, lies in the fact that many publishers have unequivocally accepted the fashionable assumption that quantity in book publishing interferes with quality. They seem to be sold on the idea that the book trade has its own Gresham's law, that bad books tend to drive out good books. Therefore they cry, privately and publicly and with more than a dash of righteousness, for fewer and better books.

This tendency to denigrate success is not peculiar to the American book industry; it is almost a shibboleth in British publishing. Readers of the *Bookseller* ("The Organ of the Book Trade in Great Britain") have long been accustomed to the editorial lamentation that has accompanied its annual report on rising statistics of British book production. And, strangely enough, the *Bookseller* has deplored, in the same vein, any annual rise in British book exports. Just think, it says with a shudder, what would happen if we should have to fall back on the home market! But the British book trade has always liked to shudder—in print—over its lot. Surely something different should be expected in the United States. Yet our own *Publishers Weekly* has been known to deplore increased production and to call sententiously for fewer and better books. (In 1974 it ran a three-part economic report on book publishing by one of its contributing editors, and a shorter critical analysis by a well-known academic economist, both of which asserted that overproduction was ruining the industry.[1]) Further, almost every Bowker Lecturer of recent years, addressing the book trade on no matter what subject, has felt constrained in passing to deplore the production of too many books. Thus the idea that quantity has tended to limit or degrade quality has been promoted by some of the sagest high priests of our industry. One of the most experienced and highly respected of all these lecturers, the late Ben Huebsch, stated his conviction in the strongest terms a few years ago.

First, Mr. Huebsch broadly asked, "Does the great increase in book production really indicate a rise in the level of our culture? Is there not a danger in overproduction as there is in overpopulation? Is there any sense in doubling the number of titles we publish to keep pace with the doubling of inhabitants of the earth?" Then, after calling on authors (not publishers) for more self-censorship, he answers his own questions unequivocally: "A consequence of the expansion of our culture should be a diminution of new books, and an end to the foolish boasting of the increase of new titles."[2]

Ben Huebsch's statement was echoed a few years later by another eminent publisher, Alfred A. Knopf, in his Bowker Lecture. While discussing his skeptical views of book advertising, Mr. Knopf said, "The publisher's advertising problem is greatly aggravated by what we have all agreed is true—too many books are published, most of them doomed in advance to a short and inglorious life. Gresham's law works here too and poor books undoubtedly tend to drive out good ones."[3]

Thus two able champions of "fewer and better books" publicly stated the popular postulate in general terms. But neither attempted to stipulate exactly why fewer books would mean better books, or just how less quantity would result in higher quality. No one ever does. So I want here to examine this postulate and challenge it from the rational, statistical, and emotional points of view. As a working principle, it is, I am convinced, as unsound as a watermelon in November.

The rationalized arguments against it are easy. For example, it is easy, and not an oversimplification, to ask: Would the novels of Eudora Welty, John Hersey, or Saul Bellow be any better if fewer third- and fourth-rate novelists were published annually? Or would the works of Thomas Pynchon, Anthony Burgess, or Bernard Malamud be improved if the number of new experimental works published each year were cut in half? Or would the publication of fewer third-rate novelists cause more of them to turn into second-raters, and more second-raters to turn into first-raters? Or, indeed, would a diminution of published fiction serve to improve the quality of published poetry, or biography, or history? Or, for an even sharper contrast, would such a diminution have any qualitative effect on the spate of titles published each year in science, technology, and the practical arts? Obviously, the answer in each case is no. Almost all authors, good or bad, professional or part-time, work as individualists, doing what they consider to be their best, giving little or no thought to the general improvement of the breed or to the general quality of the product of the writer's craft. As Granville Hicks once put it, "Fortunately, writers rarely follow the advice the critics offer them. They do what they feel they have to do, not what somebody else tells them they ought to do."

But here, the champion of "fewer and better books" will say, is where the publisher's judgment and the editor's skill should come in. But just how? Do the publisher and the editor, by stringently reducing the size of their list, thereby improve their taste and sharpen their judgment of quality? If this were true, a publishing house could grow in sales and reputation by a progressively critical reduction each year in the size of its list—which, of course, not one has ever done or is likely to do. (A favorite truism of the business is that any publishing house can improve its prestige and profit in any year by not publishing half of its list—the difficulty is in deciding which half not to publish.)

As for the editor's skill, it is often argued that if editors would only take more time and care with fewer manuscripts, the quality of published books would vastly improve. Unhappily, this idea won't wash either. In fact, the risk seems to run the other way. Given more time on fewer books, the average American book editor is likely to spend it rather on trying to make a marginal manuscript publishable than on the perfection of a manuscript that already has high quality. This is because so many of our editors have come to consider themselves as "literary doctors" and rewrite people. Most of them readily admit that they spend much too much of their time and skill trying to make silk purses out of sows' ears. And sadly enough, an occasional spectacular success, the saving of a "hopeless" manuscript, can have a lastingly bad effect on an editor's attitude toward a proper balance in the total work program.

Unlike such rationalized arguments, the emotional considerations so frequently involved in the declamation of the postulate of "fewer and better books" are subjective and highly personal, and hence much more difficult to argue. Here one must tread lightly, but treading too lightly would lose the point. So it must be observed, a bit roughly perhaps, that many publishers and editors and reviewers fold the postulate to their hearts merely because they so desperately want it to be so—the wish is father to the thought. Naturally, their sentiments appeal strongly to the idealists in the industry and to the reporters, commentators, and editorial writers who are concerned with books.

Many others sublimate the postulate into a championing of the small against the large. These are the people who argue constantly that standards of quality cannot possibly be as high in the larger "sprawling" publishing houses as in the smaller, more compact, and "personalized" houses. Naturally, many of the people who argue in this way are in the smaller houses. But many others are in the larger ones; they simply do not like bigness of any kind. Almost all of them are swayed wholly by emotion, not in the least by evidence.

In truth, there is no convincing evidence on either side of this argument. One can point to several large houses that seem to be able to maintain high standards throughout large lists published in as many as eight or ten different categories or departments. (Such a house usually operates on a decentralized pattern as a cluster of smaller houses, each having a more or less autonomous staff of competent managers and editors.) One can also find many a small house that is obviously satisfied with rather lower standards in a narrowly ranging list—and usually there is not a first-rate editor aboard. Then, without looking too hard, one can find houses, both large and small, that consistently publish lists of mixed quality, good in one field and mediocre or bad in another. This state of things is likely to continue as long as book publishing is based upon the highly personalized author-editor-publisher complex, with its almost complete dependence on subjective tastes and individual judgments. But the point here is that, contrary to a widely held and popular belief, size as such has little or nothing to do with it.

Let us suppose that the chief publishing executives of one of the larger multiple-department houses do decide in favor of fewer and better books and do want to start trimming their lists by, say, 10 percent. Obviously, they should do most or all of this trimming in the department where quality is lowest. (This does not mean, of course, that it would necessarily be the least profitable.) But they plainly see that a cut here certainly would not affect the operations of the other departments one way or the other. Publishing fewer religious books, for example, would not improve the quality of the college textbooks, nor would fewer juveniles improve the medical line. Fewer trade books would in no way affect the quality of the scientific and technical list. Each of these separate lists is selected and edited by a different group of editors, working usually under different departmental management, with a different set of quality standards and with different methods of selection and editing.

So a better way, the executives reason, might be a horizontal cut of 10 percent in every department. If their house is publishing, say, 400 titles per year in 5 departments, then they have to ask themselves: Will a reduction of each department's program by 8 titles really make the editors in that department more wise and less fallible in taste and judgment? And are the 8 excised titles likely to be much worse or better than the lowest-ranking 6 titles among the 54 accepted by each department? And are not they, the 8 excised titles, likely to be as good as, or better than, some of the best titles on many of the competitors' lists? Being at heart a philosopher and a gambler (and a publisher must be both), he or she knows the answers to these questions even before they are asked. No, this obviously would not work.

Then the thing to do is to pick out the weakest three editors in the house and fire them. This would reduce the total annual list by 10 percent. Yet, each of these three editors might still be as good as or better than the best editors in 10 or 15 other houses that are competitive in the firm's respective fields. "How," the baffled executive asks, "would this harsh course serve either our own house or the greater good of the industry?"

The hypothetical dilemma of this publishing executive brings us directly to the crux of the matter. Every publishing house, large and small, is squarely up against the fact that, as noted earlier, the book industry operates on an infinite number of individual judgments and decisions, each subjectively based on individual tastes, individual likes and dislikes, and with varying interpretations of quality requirements. The author decides to write and submit a manuscript. The editor decides to read or not to read it, then to recommend acceptance or rejection after the reading. The publisher decides to accept or reject the editor's recommendation. Usually as many as four or five individual judgments are involved in each of these decision-making complexes. Plainly, a larger number of intermediate and ultimate "noes" injected in more cases is not likely to make the "yeses" more correct in all the others. It is only when all our houses are staffed with men and women of better taste, with more knowledge and sensibility, that we shall be able to "cut out all the trash" and publish only the better books. For by final analysis the overproduction that is being so constantly deplored is nothing more nor less than the industry's normal quantum of mistakes—mistakes made in the countless number of individual author-editor-publisher decision-making complexes in our many, many publishing houses, day in and day out.

So much for rational and emotional arguments—always as easy to reject as they are to muster. Statistically based arguments are more difficult and more tedious; it is much easier to look at each year's increase of the total figure for new-book production and exclaim, "My God! How awful." But if one stops and takes a historical look at the figures behind the annual increase, it will soon be discovered that there is really no cause for despair. In fact, the figures indicate quite clearly that for many years new-book production has not kept pace with sales or with growing potential markets for books in the United States.

In the short-term view, the numbers of new and revised books published annually in the 1960s increased by 90 percent—from 14,876 titles to 29,579 titles. Then in the next five years, the number increased by 33 percent—up to 39,372 titles in 1975. The overall increase in the 15-year period was about 162 percent. (These production statistics are taken from annual reports by *Publishers Weekly*, which are not accurate as a historical index. The ground rules for their compilation have changed from time to time; for example, reprinted facsimile editions were counted as new productions for the first time in 1970, which caused an aberrational increase of 22 percent for the one year alone.[4] Further, the system at *Publishers Weekly* for gathering industry-wide information has been improved in recent years. Accordingly, the figures for post-1970 years should be substantially discounted for valid comparability with earlier years.)

By comparison, book sales in current-dollar value increased by 150 percent in the 1960s, then by 30.8 percent in the following 5-year period. The overall increase for the 15-year period was 226 percent. Thus it is apparent that new-title production, though greatly increased, has not outstripped the growth of book markets since 1960.

Further, it is significant to observe that the value of U.S. gross national product increased by 200 percent in the 15-year period, while book sales were increasing by 226 percent and new-book production by 162 percent. It is obvious, then, that the rate of new-book production has fallen short of both the rise in book sales and the overall growth of our national economy.

Nor does it seem that new-book production has kept pace with the rapid rise in the book-reader potential in the United States. In the absence of a better way to measure this potential, the number of our citizens with four or more years of college education can be accepted as a good index. In this index the numbers of college graduates rose from 8.3 million in 1959 to 13.8 million in 1969, then to 21.4 million in 1975—an increase of 159 percent in 16 years.[5] How can anyone put these figures against the comparable figures on new-book production and still cry the calamity of over-production? The real calamity, it seems, lies in the fact that book publishers have not yet learned more about how this greatly increased potential can be exploited.

What is more, the prospect of continued growth in book-reading aged populations is very bright. Demographers are predicting steady growth in the senior citizen population, which has the education, income, and leisure that correlate with book reading. And one astute observer of the demographers' forecasts, Dan Lacy of McGraw-Hill, points out that even if the current reduction in the U.S. birth rate continues, we probably shall have 30,000,000 more Americans before the end of the century. To this forecast Mr. Lacy adds:

> . . . one other major factor that will produce an upward thrust in the demand for books is the rapid growth in the relatively young, highly-educated adult population that will take place over the next two decades . . . twenty years from now there should be nearly 80,000,000 Americans in their 20's and 30's with 40,000,000 having a college education. There have never been such numbers of young, educated, relatively affluent people in any nation in the world before.[6]

One can only hope that book publishers will manage, long before the end of the century, to overcome their ingrained and inane fear of growth to match their potential markets.

11

A Sea Change
in Subject Publishing

To argue the generality of overproduction in the book industry is really a waste of time. The real heart of the matter lies in these specific questions: Just where has increased production most occurred? In what subject categories and in what segments of the industry? In what kinds of books for what classes of readers?

In approaching these questions one must remember that book publishing is a varied and highly segmented industry. Trade-book publishers produce many kinds of books on many, many subjects, and so do textbook publishers. Neither has much interest in common with the other, nor much influence, if any, on the other. Publishers in such fields as law, medicine, business, religion, and science and technology live and produce in worlds of their own, with little or no reference to the world of general books. The same can be said of other specialists, such as the publishers of children's books and of encyclopedias.

Now, just where in all this diversified complex of the book industry have the greatest increases in new titles occurred? In order to get at specific answers to this question, I have kept a historical tab on the annual reports of Bowker's *Weekly Record* as a measure of the comparative growth of two large categories of books. This record, which goes back to 1929, shows a remarkable sea change in the complexion of subject matter of American book publishing since that year.

For the want of better labels, I have called one category "Literary Books" and the other "Practical and Professional Books." This particular division was made because I am sure that most proponents of the "too-many-books" postulate would protest, saying, "But we were not talking about practical and professional books, or handbooks, or textbooks, or how-to-do-it books and such, many of which probably shouldn't be called books at all." (I have heard statements such as this made to bookish audiences, who never fail to gurgle approval.) But they must be talking about this kind of book, for the record shows that the Practical and Professional category accounts for the larger part by far of the total increase in new-book production over the 46-year period. Actually, the number of Practical and Professional books published in 1975 was 625 percent over 1929, while the number of Literary Books was only 119 percent higher. The accompanying tabulations, which show four decades of growth plus the six-year period 1969–1975, reveal some significant growth patterns by subject classification within the two categories.

The most provocative trend shown in the tables is the increase in published fiction in the past 15 years, a period in which originally published novels have been almost stone dead in the marketplace. The answer to this riddle lies, of course, in the increased support of fiction by magazine and newspaper serialization and by book clubs and other reprinters. Americans are increasingly reading novels in reprint form; and, as noted earlier, most American publishers are now relying mainly on reprint income for whatever profits they may be able to derive from fiction.

Another remarkable growth pattern is seen in scientific and technical books. From the production figures for these subjects, it would seem that the publishers of such books would be the ones

LITERARY BOOKS PUBLISHED ANNUALLY—BY SUBJECT[1]

Subject	1929	1939	1949	1959	1969	1975
Biography	738	628	595	776	1,161	1,968
Fiction	2,142	1,547	1,644	2,437	2,717	3,805
General Literature	572	584	535	836	724	1,904
Poetry and Drama	727	657	574	499	1,254	1,501
	4,179	3,416	3,348	4,548	5,856	9,178

(Increase 1975 over 1929: 4,999 titles, or 119 percent.)

PRACTICAL AND PROFESSIONAL BOOKS PUBLISHED ANNUALLY—BY SUBJECT

Subject	1929	1939	1949	1959	1969	1975
Agriculture	82	129	191	129	260	456
Business	213	357	306	422	683	820
Education	317	315	254	417	842	1,038
Sports and Games	130	219	235	259	734	1,225
Home Economics	53	148	263	181	314	728
Law	116	160	267	302	525	915
Medicine	402	431	450	590	1,190	2,282
Sociology and Economics	484	854	548	625	4,462	6,590
Science	424	523	676	1,033	2,353	2,924
Technology	359	461	455	736	1,035	1,720
	2,580	3,597	3,645	4,694	12,398	18,698

(Increase 1975 over 1929: 16,118 titles, or 625 percent.)

to cry in anguish for fewer books. But not so. These publishers think their sharply stepped-up production rate is just dandy. They are, in fact, having to scramble to keep up with their exploding subject matter and their almost limitless publishing opportunities.

Speaking of the flourishing of science and scientific publishing suggests a pause here to give an answer to Mr. Huebsch's earlier question. "Does the increase in book production really indicate a rise in the level of our culture?" I would answer, "Yes, it does. And, moreover, it indicates a change, a basic and sweeping change, in the pattern of our culture." This change has come in recent years with the new scientific revolution—a change that was brilliantly described by Sir C. P. Snow in his *The Two Cul-*

tures and the Scientific Revolution.[2] The importance and the consequences of this change are almost wholly ignored by publishers who know only the "literary" side of publishing. They fail to see that this revolution has caused a sweeping change in the publishing pattern to fit the changing cultural pattern. Sadly enough, as Sir Charles noted, the tradition-bound adherents of our literary culture only bury their heads in their hands and refuse to look when the change is pointed out to them.

Another burgeoning segment of publishing from which one hears no complaint is juvenile books. Here the annual recorded production of new titles increased by 33 percent in the years 1960–1975 and dollar sales also increased by 44 percent! I cite this record of the past 15 years because it spanned the relentless rise of television, which supposedly usurped all our children's time. And it happened while many authorities, both professional and amateur, were telling us over and over again that Johnny can't read, and wouldn't even if he could. Naturally, the publishers of juveniles wonder, not unhappily, if Johnny isn't reading all these books, who is?

There are several other categories that have expanded rapidly in both number of titles and sales volume, including fine arts and music, both of which again owe much to the influence of television. History is still another, but here one cannot trace so surely the influence of TV. At any rate, enough has been said, I think, to support the point that the book industry has grown far beyond its traditional hard-core interest in creative literature, and that most of the expansion has come in fields that are not a part of our traditional literary culture. This the bewailers, the callers for fewer and better books, have failed to perceive. And they have also failed to perceive that their bewailing is quite harmful to the book industry as a whole.

Just how is it harmful? First, it encourages book review editors and their reviewers, along with librarians and booksellers, to feel that they are being more and more swamped every year by ever-higher floods of books with which they cannot possibly cope. Theirs is a natural feeling, but why should publishers help to exaggerate it? Other occupational and professional classes have learned how to cope with increases of products or services that have run far higher than those of the book industry. Are the reviewers, librarians, and booksellers really justified in their constant, and constantly encouraged, complaint on this score?

Second, the bewailers encourage—even invite—the general public to believe that the book industry is knowingly producing and palming off each year a lot of superfluous trash—trash that would surely be eliminated if only the apostles of fewer and better books had their way. Certainly it is unfortunate that the whole industry should have to bear such a slander by those who appear to be indulging the purely personal and senseless satisfactions of breast-beating.

It seems, then, that publishers should put a damper on their histrionics, should stop talking so loosely in broad generalities, and should face more realistically the changes in the world for which they publish. Would it not make sense for all of us to call in unison for more and better books of all kinds for anybody and everybody who wants them?

Here I must caution that nothing in the foregoing disquisition is intended to suggest that publishers don't have a constant obligation to maintain the highest possible level of quality in their lists. This they must always strive to do—for themselves, for their industry, for the booksellers, and for book buyers everywhere. In so doing, they must, of course, resolutely discourage mediocre talent and firmly reject manuscripts of doubtful value— but not in *all* cases. This is to say that all publishers must now and then compromise their principles to meet the realities of existing circumstances—which they soon learn to do comfortably enough if they are astute enough.

For, assuredly, the control of literary pollution is neither a simple nor an easy task, not for even the most experienced publisher. Too many subjective values are involved, too many differentials of need and taste must be considered, to permit easy decisions. In what other area is one man's meat so often another man's poison? And just what set of objective critical standards can be applied to gauge the literary and substantive qualities of books of so many different varieties?

Recognizing the subtle difficulties of their day-to-day judgmental tasks, wise publishers try their best to keep loose and eclectic and generous in their decisions on what to publish and what to reject. And when they are wise enough, they will actually pay little attention to the pietistic shibboleth of fewer and better books. This is because they know that few writers consistently produce works of high quality, that few publishers have the ability to attract and select only the best of manuscripts, and that very few readers want constantly to read only books of the highest literary and intellectual quality. Honestly recognizing these facts of life, true-blue publishers do what they can within realistic limits to give a consistently high level of general quality to their lists each season. They realize that they must occasionally publish middling or even mediocre books in order to bring along promising authors. Most authors do not produce their best work until after they have published at least one or two books of which they may be ashamed later. So what would happen if authors were not published until they are matured writers of first-rate books? This question is ignored by those high-minded publishers and critics who continually call for the elimination of all but high-quality works from the publishers' crowded lists each year. These would-be reformers of the book industry blink the fact that the production of flawed and faltering books nearly always plays a formative part in the education and development of an author—that such books often are the stepping stones to literary excellence.

Further, all successful publishers learn in time that they have to come to terms with the public taste and preference in reading matter. As noted, most readers do not like highbrow books as a steady diet; for a change they will often turn to middlebrow and even lowbrow books for relaxing and restful enjoyment—to detective stories, to shoddy romantic or sexy novels, to sensationalized biographies, to gossipy, tattletale memoirs, and the like. Thus the public taste will be served, and sensible publishers recognize the fact that mediocre books often have educational value to readers also. Mystery stories and cheap novels and sensationalized biographies can also serve as stepping stones to appreciation of much better literature. So it seems that such books should not be too much denigrated and despised. And, indeed, even the best publishers have to admit in honesty that they will now and then publish books whose potential sales appeal far outshines either their literary merit or intellectual worth.

There are, of course, those who argue that trashy books serve to debase the public taste. This is a highly questionable postulate. For my part, I believe that the public taste has been debased through all of recorded history, and that it has slowly but surely improved by building from the mediocre and the middling to the better and the best. What is more, I believe that our movies and TV programs, as bad as they are, will help in time to uplift the public taste. This implies, of course, that the public taste still is very low indeed. So it is, and that is why the book—almost any kind of book—will somehow serve to elevate it. Samuel Johnson, in an age when the public taste in England was about as low as one can imagine, declared that he would let a boy "at first read *any* English book which happens to engage his attention; because you have done a great deal when you have brought him to entertainment from a book. He'll get better books afterwards."

12

Of Mergers, Miscegenation, and Synergism

Another, but not so subtle, phenomenon of change occurred in the book industry in the 1960s. This was the movement for corporate mergers and for takeovers between the electronics-communications industry and book publishers. It resulted in a good number of "cross-media" marriages, many of them miscegenetic. Most were inspired by rationalized dreams of synergistically induced extra-dividend happiness on the electronics industry side, and were encouraged by the book industry's need for more working capital and for established market value of the stocks of many privately owned book companies. Under these conditions, several industrial giants (hardware grooms) happily took to wife many carefully selected bedmates among the available book firms (software brides). "We have the hardware, they have the software," said General Sarnoff when RCA acquired Random House in 1966. With the same kind of concupiscence flowing hot in their corporate veins, General Electric joined Time, Inc., in organizing the General Learning Corporation, with the textbook house Silver Burdette as the software base. And, within the decade, CBS acquired Holt, Rinehart and Winston, Allyn & Bacon, and W. B. Saunders Company; IBM bought Science Research Associates; Xerox bought Ginn and Company and R. R. Bowker; Raytheon purchased D. C. Heath, and Litton Industries took over an assortment of houses, including D. Van Nostrand and American Book Company.

All these miscegenetic marriages were widely celebrated in the press as presaging a new day for the communications and learning media. This caused the value of all "independent" book houses to soar with the generally escalating stock market prices to the end of the decade. But the trend was greatly feared by many in the book industry—they were sure it would over-commercialize book publishing and might even defile the purity of the printed volume.

It is interesting to observe, parenthetically, that much of this excitement over the synergistic potentials and the growth prospects of book publishing as a part of the so-called knowledge industry can be traced to a rather dry academic study produced in 1962 by Professor Fritz Machlup, then at Princeton University. Entitled *The Production and Distribution of Knowledge in the United States*,[1] this study was a loose, catchall economic analysis in which a complexity of statistical relationships was stated but never clearly correlated or validated. The correlations often were only suggested, and the potentials for synergistic effects were more implied than stated. The author was careful to warn his readers of these imperfections in his study, but the warning was, unfortunately, more often ignored than heeded. In any case, Professor Machlup's study was hastily taken as unqualified glad tidings by many journalists and Wall Street analysts, whose secondary reports sparked a gold rush for book publishers' equities, a rush that would last to the end of the decade.

As things turned out, the book industry's anxiety over the spate of mergers in the 1960s was baseless. A few of them worked out very well, but more were tried and found wanting. The highly touted synergetic effects did not come off as expected; the hardware-software unions were disappointingly unproductive of profitable hybrids. Clearly, electronics and books have not mixed so readily and effectively as many people believed they would. Consequently, some high-powered grooms have been heard to grumble about their brides, most of which were bought at fancy prices. At the same time, many low-powered book publishers have unexpectedly been enjoying life as millionaires. So, by the end of the decade, the miscegenetic marriages had lost much of their glamour. Later, the General Learning Corporation complex was annulled and dissolved as a union, and several software brides were spun off at reduced prices, mostly to independent publishers who would try to rehabilitate their original purity. In passing, it should be noted that the hardware-software mergers that have worked happily are the ones in which the synergism strategy has not been pushed too hard against natural limitations. Notable examples of wholly owned publishing subsidiaries that have continued to thrive after mergers are Random House under RCA ownership and Howard W. Sams & Co. Inc., under ITT ownership.

So it has become obvious that the many mergers and cross-media marriages will not result, as widely supposed, in a baneful concentration of book publishing in the hands of a few large and powerful corporate complexes and conglomerates. To be sure, many independent houses, large and small, have become operating units in a variety of much larger corporate structures, where some of them have taken on new life. But, at the same time, many new and growing firms have come along to take their places in the ranks of the independents. In fact, contrary to popular belief, these ranks have been more than filled every year. Actually, there are many more independent book houses in the United States today than at the start of the wave of mergers and takeovers. As noted earlier, Bowker's *Literary Market Place* listed over 1,000 imprints in 1976 compared with 585 listed 16 years earlier in the 1960 edition. It seems, then, that the book industry certainly was never in danger of being gobbled up or monopolized by a few large and sinister industrial octopuses.

Yet, in keeping with trends in U.S. business and industry generally (and often for the same reasons and exigencies that existed in the 1960s), mergers continued at a steady pace in the 1970s. Most of them involved small companies, seeking strength through combined resources. Others, but only a few, were combinations of larger houses, or acquisitions of smaller firms by larger firms. Actually, the *Bowker Annual*[2] for 1977 reported a total of 17 book-imprint mergers and acquisitions in 1976. But only three of these could be considered of major importance: Dell's merger with Doubleday; MCA-Universal's purchase of G. P. Putnam's Sons, Berkley Publishing Corporation, and Coward, McCann & Geoghegan; and CBS's acquisition of Fawcett Publications.

Nevertheless, the trend continues to be marked enough (and publicized enough by reporters who are avid for "gobbling-up" news slants) that it worries authors who think their prospects for publication are being seriously diminished. Their complaints have excited the interest of the Department of Justice and the Federal Trade Commission on the grounds of possible restraint of trade. Consequently it appears, as this book goes to press, that official investigations may come eventually. If they do come, the publishers will surely suffer substantial losses of time and money in defense of their position, and the uneasy symbiosis with their authors will become even more uneasy. In my view, it appears unlikely that the authors' very general and amorphous charges can be supported by factual evidence. Indeed, I doubt if there ever has been a time in U.S. publishing history when the author of a worthy manuscript has had a better chance of finding a worthy publisher.

13

Will Paperbacks
Take Over?

Since the general public is exposed far more widely to mass-market paperbacks than to hardcover books, it is natural that most people would have an exaggerated notion of the relative importance of paperback publishing to the U.S. book industry *in toto*. In fact, a good part of the public—and especially the youth sector—seems to think that paperback books have taken over, that it will be only a matter of time until all books are published in cheap paper-covered editions. A well-known publisher recently reported his shock at hearing his grandson say, "I don't know why anybody would buy a high-priced hardcover book when anything worth reading can soon be bought as a paperback." Even further misled was an ebullient *New York Times* reporter who started his recent "news analysis" report on the current state of the book industry by saying that publishers could wish that hardcover books would go away and stay, because nowadays satisfactory sales and profits are derived only from paperback reprints. How wrong are such uninformed views!

Actually, mass-market paperback publishing has never had anything like a predominant position in the industry. While its growth has been rapid (if somewhat erratic) in the past decade, its dollar sales volume has never been more than 8 to 10 percent of the industry's total, and its share of profits has been much lower. This is, of course, purely an economic evaluation of size and importance within the book industry. In terms of the reading public's interest, as translated into numbers of copies sold, the evaluation is very different. Since the net price of the average mass-market paperback is about one-tenth that of the average hardcover book, it follows that the unit sales (number of copies) of paperbacks each year almost equal those of hardcover volumes. Further, a faster rate of sales increase has been enjoyed by mass-market paperbacks than by adult hardbound books. For the period 1971–1976, the increases were 81.6 and 35.6 percent respectively.

At the same time, another kind of paperback edition has rapidly increased its relatively small share of the total book market. These are the so-called quality paperbacks (or adult trade paperbound books) that are published, or republished, in relatively large printings and priced for popular-demand markets at 30 to 50 percent of the prices of comparable hardbound books. Some are published originally in paper covers only, others in dual editions simultaneously in cloth and paper covers. (Many basic textbooks also are now published in the same way.) The sale of adult paperbound books increased by 69 percent in the five-year period 1971–1976; still their share of the total dollar sales was less than 4 percent at the end of the period.

It is obvious, then, that paperback publishing is not about to dominate the book industry. Indeed, barring revolutions in reading habits and in book-manufacturing technology, it seems unlikely that papercover editions will ever be suitable for run-of-the-mill books—meaning about 90 percent of those published annually. There are several reasons for this, all of which are conveniently ignored by paperback enthusiasts who let their wish be father to their thought.

The prime reason is the simple matter of production cost in relation to the potential market for a book. For the original edition of most kinds of books, the total cost of producing it in hard covers is only slightly more than in paper covers. The difference is slight because the composition, printing, and paper costs are the same no matter what kind of cover is put on. Further, a large part of the cost of the binding process—that of folding, gathering, and trimming the sheets—is the same. Thus it is only the costs of the binding materials, of the sewing of sheets, and of the casing-in process that can be higher or lower. Actually, the cost of producing a $10.00 book (in a first printing of 10,000 copies) with a hard cover is only 25 or 30 cents more than that of the same book with a paper cover. Considering this slight difference in total manufacturing costs, one can readily understand why most books are not originally published as paperbacks.

Another production cost factor is the high editorial and plant costs of many, many books, such as medical, scientific, technical, and certain kinds of specialized reference titles. For such books the high first-copy cost cannot possibly be recovered by selling at quality-paperback prices in limited markets. In other words, high unit prices are required to cover the high fixed costs that come with short-run printings.

One thing that confuses the public in its awareness of the wide difference between the prices of paperback and hardbound books is the publisher's ambiguous practice in pricing simultaneously published dual editions. Customarily, the hardbound edition is overpriced and the paperback edition is substantially underpriced, and the publisher hopes to regain by additional sales what is lost on the low profit margin of the paperback edition. Often it does not work this way. In any event, the hardcover edition usually is produced to satisfy the demand of the many libraries that will not buy paperback books. But the general public is not aware of these facts, nor indeed are many librarians.

The foregoing comparison of the costs of paperbound and clothbound books is not intended to imply a similarly narrow gap between the cost of a clothbound original edition and that of a typical mass-market paperback reprint edition. Rather, it is meant to suggest the answer to the often-heard query as to why textbooks and professional and reference books cannot be produced and sold in very cheap paperback editions. It must be emphasized that the mass-market paperback reprint is altogether a different economic package. Its editorial and composition costs are negligible; the quality of its printing and manufacturing materials is very low; its market has been established by the original edition, so it can safely be printed in quantities ranging up into tens or hundreds of thousands of copies. In short, the economy of scale of its production is of a very different order of magnitude.

Publishers often hear another question about paperbacks: Are they replacing the conventional "monolithic" textbook? Here the answer must be carefully hedged because paperbacks have, in fact, become widely used for instruction at almost all colleges and universities and at many high schools as well. It appears, however, that in most instances they have rather supplemented than supplanted the required basic text or book of readings. Still, in a few areas of instruction, and notably in English and certain humanistic courses, they have indeed often supplanted basic texts—a fact that has been widely bruited in academic circles and widely advertised, naturally, by paperback publishers. But for the large majority of courses (and especially for those in the exact and applied sciences and in vocational and preprofessional training) the conventional textbook has lost very little ground to paperbacks—unless, of course, the ground has been lost occasionally to textbooks split into "instructional units" and cloaked in paper covers.

Further, while I am on the subject, it seems safe to predict that the conventional textbook will continue to be a necessary fixture of American education for some years to come. Educational book publishers know, perhaps better than anyone else, the reasons why this is so. They have seen the textbook continue to flourish through many years of vilification and disdain as being a blight on the nation's educational system. So they have long since become completely callous to the intellectual loftiness of those teachers who like to proclaim that the lowly textbook is a bane to their profession. Educational publishers see that the large majority of teachers have not enough intellectual discipline or organizational ability to do their jobs well without that convenient "crutch," the well-organized textbook. Publishers see, too, that very few educational institutions have adequate library facilities to support courses organized wholly on the lecture/reference principle, even if teachers generally could so organize them. Even more importantly, publishers know that as long as advancement through our educational system is measured in units (academic credits) of acquired knowledge, the textbook will remain a very efficient and highly desired instructional tool—this because it responds so nicely to the requirement of the system for neatly packaged units of learning. For this reason alone, it is unlikely that the conventional textbook will lose its often disparaged popularity unless and until there is a radical change in the American educational system itself.

Returning to the current state of paperback publishing, one can note a ferment of questioning and questing as to how reprint rights can best be handled by individual houses. When the rising star of Pocket Books reprint editions first came over the horizon in the 1940s, everyone assumed that reprinting for mass markets was a highly specialized kind of publishing that should best be left with the specialists. And so it was for about two decades. Almost all hardcover publishers were content to sell reprint rights in their backlists and current best-sellers to Pocket Books, or to one of the few other pioneers in the expanding field, which included Dell, Fawcett, Bantam, Popular Library, and New American Library.

But as paperback publishing continued to grow, and as reprints of many books (including some undistinguished or even disgusting ones) began to sell by the millions of copies, some houses had second thoughts on the matter. Why, they asked themselves, should we not cash in on the reprint potentials of our own books? If the "paperback explosion" is to produce the "wave of the future" (as one journalist put it), why shouldn't we ride it ourselves? With these thoughts in mind, and possessing the resources to establish mass-marketing facilities, several larger firms either started their own reprint lines or acquired going paperback houses. Thus Doubleday established Anchor Books and Image Books; Harper & Row established Chapel Books and Torchbooks; Houghton Mifflin established Sentry Editions and Riverside Editions; Harcourt Brace Jovanovich established Harvest Books and acquired Pyramid Books; Random House established Vintage Books and acquired Ballantine; Viking established Compass Books; etc. In some conglomerates, hardcover and paperback houses operated in tandem under a single ownership: Putnam's and Berkley Publishing Corporation are both owned by MCA, Inc., and Holt, Rinehart and Winston and Popular Library both operate in the CBS publishing group. In spite of these "in-house" or "bedfellow" arrangements, all the larger hardcover publishers continue to sell reprint rights to specialized softcover publishers, and in most cases the wholly owned reprinters continue to produce titles acquired from outside houses. Thus the marketplace for attractive reprint rights has been free-wheeling, free-dealing, and highly competitive.

Indeed, some reprint houses have thought that the competition for reprint rights has been too healthy in recent years. They have seen many such rights in best-sellers sold at auction for amounts running high into hundred-thousand-dollar figures each, and lately sales at more than one million have not been uncommon. Disliking the auction squeeze, a few of the large reprinters have thought to avoid it by establishing their own hardcover imprints as a ploy for enticing established best-seller authors directly into their own houses. Thus, Dell, Bantam, and New American Library, all with large resources, have tried their hands at original publishing through very lucrative hardcover/reprint "package" contracts with carefully selected authors. To date, each has scored a few impressive successes, but the strategy has not been as broadly effective as its planners hoped for. Even so, the idea should not be faulted too quickly.

Most observers have read significant signs of change into the announcements of two very recent mergers that involved large paperback publishers. The first came in 1975 when Penguin Books, the oldest and largest of British reprint houses, bought Viking Press, one of the most successful and prestigious of American trade-book firms. This particular merger was both unusual and surprising on two counts: first, that a paperback firm would acquire a sizable hardcover firm; second, that a British house would buy an American house. (In the vernacular, this was indeed a turning of the tables!) The second provocative merger came in 1976 when Doubleday & Company, the largest of American trade-book houses, acquired Dell Publishing Company, one of the largest and most successful of American reprint houses. In this merger, the size and power of the two firms were enough alone to cause a sensation in the book world. The fact that it was a top-drawer combination of hardcover and paperback interests added spice to the speculation about its meaning. Also, it added considerably to the concern of some authors and authors' organizations over what they think of as "captive" in-house transfers of reprint rights. They fear that such transfers, or the sales of reprint rights by parent hardcover companies to their softcover reprint subsidiaries, can reduce competition for paperback rights and thus the prices at which sales are made are lowered and the concomitant immediate income to authors is reduced. This point was made in their complaints to the Department of Justice and the Federal Trade Commission, referred to in the preceding chapter.

Presumably, some pressing financial and tax considerations were involved in each of the unusual mergers just described. Still, one has to assume that each signified high-level convictions that paperback publishing is "the perdurable force" in the trade-book world of today. The quoted phrase was recently used by an eminent publisher, William Jovanovich, in describing his reason for combining the editorial staffs of the trade-book and paper-back divisions of Harcourt Brace Jovanovich, Inc. Mr. Jovanovich started by saying that he found it no longer possible to make money on hardcover trade books before subsidiary rights are sold. Then he expressed the hope that the change in editorial management would create a better distribution system for the firm's trade books, and would also facilitate the decision process in choosing how a manuscript should be published—in hard-cover only, in hardcover and paperback simultaneously, in trade paperbacks only, or in mass-market paperback only. Further, he thought the house should be in a better position to calculate whether a book should remain on the hardcover backlist, or should be licensed for reprint by another firm, or should be reprinted in-house. "All these options should be an organic part of one publishing department," Mr. Jovanovich concluded.[1]

Judging from what may be inferred from the foregoing recital of developments and events, it seems that paperback publishing has not yet settled into any fixed mode or mold. The situation is dynamic and plastic, and it still is inviting and challenging to further innovation. So, though paperbacks are not about to take over the book world, they certainly do offer exciting potentials for further change and growth.

14

Copyright:
The Key to Survival

Copyright is another area where book publishers have been historically neglectful of their own interests. The industry's concern for the importance of copyright protection was unbelievably lax in the first years of the congressional effort to overhaul the country's antiquated copyright law—an effort that started in earnest in the early 1960s and ended with the enactment of the Copyright Revision Act of 1976. All but a few publishers were slow in awakening to the potential danger of several proposed changes in the law that were intended to lower the general level of protection that had existed since the enactment of the Copyright Act of March 3, 1909. And even when a rude awakening finally came, the industry's general reaction was both uninformed and inept. Indeed, it was not until the long-drawnout battle over several critical issues was all but lost that publishers finally managed to organize an effective defense. But it was a rearguard defense to the end, and not more than one publisher in ten took an active part in it.

Since copyright is universally recognized as the sine qua non of private-enterprise publishing, how can this indifference and lethargy be explained? Several perceivable and plausible reasons can be proffered.

First, very few publishing executives really understood the plural nature of copyright protection as it had long existed under the statutory law and the court-made law of the United States. It was easy to stand off from something so arcane and difficult, and something that had worked quite well, thank you, through the first half of the century.

Second, most publishers did not perceive the legal distinction between intellectual property and real property—how the law allows certain kinds of public uses of the former that are not allowed of the latter. Too many of us thought that both kinds of rights were equally exclusive, absolute, and secure.

Third, in almost all publishing houses, copyright problems had traditionally been turned over to the firm's legal staff or to outside counsel. Let the lawyers cope—that was what they were paid for.

Fourth, most publishers had very little knowledge of, or interest in, the legislative process. We failed to understand the intricate, adversary ways in which most laws are fashioned and enacted by Congress.

Fifth, far too many publishing executives habitually expected the staff of their trade association to take care of difficult problems in Washington, including copyright. Again, that was what they were paid to do.

Sixth, far too many of us failed to perceive how much the many advances in communications technology that came at mid-century had outmoded the ancient Copyright Act of 1909. We were too busy doing our conventional thing to pay due attention to the new generations of reprographic and electron-optical devices that suddenly were coming into wide commercial use.

Of these assorted reasons, the first, second, and last best explain the indifference of the industry to the revision legislation as it was developed through the 1960s. Many publishers were smug, even arrogant, in their attitude toward the proposed changes in the law. Alas, some of us did not know even enough about copyright to realize that it is a discretionary, not an absolute, constitutional right. We were not even familiar with Article I, Section 8 of the Constitution, which reads: "The Congress shall have Power . . . to promote the Progress of Science and useful Arts, by securing for limited Times to Authors and Inventors the exclusive Right to their respective Writings and Discoveries." Had we been better informed and more astute, we would have seen that under this constitutional provision the basic purpose of copyright is to promote the public welfare, not to protect private interests—though the latter is implied as necessary for the former. And we would have realized that rights can be taken away at any time by the Congress in accordance with its current concept of what is best in the public interest. We learned the hard way about the uncertain and mutable nature of copyright law. Also, we learned that several influential classes of users of copyrighted works had, and continue to have, the determined view that copyright is a baneful monopoly that should be diminished in every possible way.

In short, the U.S. book industry learned some bitter lessons and saw the copyright principle seriously mauled in the debates over the several revision bills that were introduced and reintroduced in Congress in the 1960s and the first half of the 1970s. Nor were the book publishers alone in their early indifference to the maulings. Newspaper and magazine publishers were even more indifferent and uninformed, and they never did rally effectively to the defense of the common cause. In fact, almost all the burden of defense by the print media fell, in the end, upon book publishers. Many publishers of scientific and scholarly journals (mostly professional societies) gave what help they could, but the publishers of commercial newspapers and magazines remained appallingly unconcerned and inactive. Only a very few of them even took notice of the issues and of the protracted and often shrill debates in Washington.

As it turned out, the Copyright Revision Act of 1976, most of which is effective January 1, 1978, was not as prejudicial to the interests of authors and publishers as it might have been. Indeed, most publishers welcomed the long-delayed enactment of the bill. It was the first general overhaul of the statutory law that dated back to the 1909 code, much of which had been archaic and troublesome for many years. Still the new act was greeted more with a sigh of relief than with a sense of elation. While several important points were gained on the side of protection, some critical ground was lost to the advocates of exempted uses and of government regulation of such uses. To some of us who had long been in the thick of the legislative battle, it appeared that the book industry probably had lost more than it had gained—but, of course, only time will tell how the balance between producers and users of copyrighted works will eventually be affected.[1]

Although the 1976 act was generally labeled as a "publisher's law," it is actually more of an author's law in its general impact. The legislative report stated explicitly that the purpose of the new law is "to insure that authors receive the encouragement they need to create and the remuneration they fairly deserve for their creations." Thus, authors' rights are strengthened in several important respects, and most of these carry over to the benefit of publishers as well.

Of first importance among the benefits to authors is the elimination of the awkward dual system of "common law" copyright for unpublished works and of "statutory" copyright for published works. Under the 1976 act, a single system of Federal statutory copyright is established, and authors' rights are enforceable with national uniformity. This eliminated the difficulty of protecting the author's common law rights in unpublished works under laws that differ from state to state.

Further, unpublished works are protected from the time of their "creation"—and creation occurs when a work is "fixed" in copy for the first time. Thus the requirement of legal "publication" for statutory protection no longer obtains, and this greatly reduces the importance of a pivotal technical definition of what constitutes publication of a work.

The new law, as did the old, makes deposit of most finished works at the Library of Congress mandatory, but copyright registration is not required for protection. In most cases, however, deposit can be combined with registration, but an author's copyright is not lost through failure to register the work. This new provision greatly strengthens the author's legal, as well as moral, rights in a created work.

Of much importance among the gains for authors, and for publishers as well, is an extension of the term of copyright from a maximum of 56 years (28 years, plus the right of renewal for another 28 years) to the lifetime of the author plus 50 years. Besides the benefits of the longer term to authors and their heirs (and also to publishers), this change has two secondary benefits: It matches the terms of copyright in most of the other major publishing countries of the world, and thus brings the U.S. law into conformity with international standards; and it causes all of an author's work to fall into the public domain at the same time, thus doing away with the problem of determining dates of original publication.

The new law also protects the author's right to recapture publishing rights in a work that has been licensed to and copyrighted by a publisher. Under the old law, this right reverted to the author at the end of the first 28-year period of copyright because the author had the right of renewal for the second 28-year period unless this right had been specifically assigned on first publication. Under the new law, an author who grants his publisher the right to publish a work for the full term of life plus 50 years can terminate the publishing contract at the end of 40 years from its date or 35 years from the date of publication, whichever is earlier. This provision is properly designed to compensate authors for the right they lost under the renewal arrangement, but it is ambiguous as to its application to works that are already in their renewal terms.

Another important point was won for both authors and publishers on the question of legislating "fair use" of copyrighted materials. The old law was silent on the matter, and several earlier efforts to enact a workable amendment covering generally accepted limitations on the author's exclusive right of reprint had failed. In these circumstances, a widely applied doctrine of fair use had evolved judicially through a large, wide-ranging body of case law, and questions had to be settled by the courts in each instance of legal challenge. Naturally, many users of copyrighted materials, including educators, scholars, researchers, librarians, and operators of mechanized information systems, were unhappy with this situation, and they demanded that the new law be explicit on the subject. These demands were opposed by publishers and others who had practical and professional knowledge of the problem, including lawyers and legislators.

They were convinced that fair use is susceptible to neither exact definition nor workable legislation. In the end, by way of compromise between the two views, the new law explicitly recognized the principle of fair use and stated four criteria as guidance to the courts in deciding cases based on the question. Thus copyright proprietors successfully avoided what would have been, to them, a simplistic and harmful solution of a very critical problem.

Still another important gain to authors and publishers—and to book buyers as well—is the provision for the elimination of the so-called manufacturing clause from the copyright law. This clause was first introduced into the U.S. law in the 1890s as a form of protection for the U.S. printing industry. It specified that no book by an American author could be manufactured abroad and imported into the United States in more than a limited number of copies without the loss of copyright protection. In earlier years, the limit was 1,000 copies; in more recent years, it was 1,500 copies. This law has long been opposed in publishing circles on the principle that copyright was being used as an instrument of foreign trade regulation, but the U.S. printing industry and the printing trades unions were strong enough to block all attempts at its repeal. However, the new law liberalizes the restrictions on book manufacturing abroad for the period January 1, 1978, to July 1, 1982. In this period, 2,000 copies of a foreign-manufactured book may be imported, and copyright is not lost if that number is exceeded. (The copyright owner loses protection only against an infringer of publishing rights.) At the end of this interim period, all manufacturing restrictions will end entirely. This long-overdue event will bring lower costs and prices for several kinds of books, but the benefits will not be as great as they might have been ten or twenty years ago. Alas, book-manufacturing costs in many foreign countries (Japan, Holland, Germany, Italy, and the United Kingdom) are now almost as high as they are in the United States.

It is more difficult to assess the losses suffered by authors and publishers in the prolonged and tortuous legislative process that produced the act of 1976. Some of them are so philosophical and subtle in nature that they can only be taken collectively as a general dilution of the principle of copyright protection. For example, the act contains four different provisions for compulsory licensing of copyrighted works where only one had existed before. This increased the government's regulatory role and produced a statutory tribunal for bureaucratic rate making for several kinds of public-interest use of protected works. (Compulsory licensing means that anyone is free to make specified uses of certain kinds of copyrighted materials without permission, provided that certain government-established or tribunal-fixed fees are paid to copyright owners. Authors lose the right to control the use of their works, and neither an author nor a publisher can grant anyone an exclusive license for a specified purpose or period.) Although some of the provisions for compulsory licensing do not apply to written works, many authors and publishers view these changes as being the beginning, perhaps, of a serious intrusion of "Big Government" on copyright protection as it had been enjoyed for many decades in our private enterprise system of publishing in the United States.

Another area where authors and publishers lost ground under the provisions of the new law is the permitted uses of photocopies for classroom and interlibrary loan purposes. While the law itself places reasonable limitations on such uses, the limitations depend, in actual practice, on two sets of extralegal guidelines that were worked out by the opposing parties for and against the proposed two kinds of exemptions. Unfortunately, both of these sets of guidelines are so intricate and so inexact as to invite disrespect or evasion by the thousands upon thousands of technically uninformed teachers and librarians who are supposed to observe them. Moreover, conformity with the guidelines requires the keeping of specific records of materials photocopied, a burden that most libraries cannot be expected to assume willingly and faithfully.[2] It seems then, that these sections of the law will need additional guidelines that are far more simple and clear and enforceable. Also, it seems inevitable that these sections will give rise to many test cases for the establishment of court law under the new act. It goes without saying that such litigation is bound to cause continued contention and bitterness between authors and publishers on the one hand and librarians, teachers, and researchers on the other. This is a shame, but here the opposing parties seem to be unable to do as Shakespeare advised adversaries in law to do: "Strive mightily, but eat and drink as friends." The issues have become too firm and the adversaries are now too hardened for that.

In passing the Copyright Revision Act of 1976, the Ninety-fourth Congress left for later action several urgent copyright issues that have considerable importance to many book publishers. These have to do with the storage and retrieval of copyrighted materials in computer-based information systems, with the protection of proprietary information files and computer application programs, with transmission and rediffusion by communications satellites, and with certain commercial relationships between the owners and the users of information transferred by the new electron-optical devices.

Dealing with these more unfamiliar and arcane issues will be very difficult for both the Congress and the parties who have conflicting interests at stake in each area. Hence, it is predictable that the copyright pot will continue to boil for some years to come. In this foreseeable situation, the book industry cannot afford to relax its vigilance. Although the postponed legislation for the regulation of technological uses may not in all instances affect the interests of producers of copyrighted printed matter, such legislation will be sure to have important bearings on the basic question of balance between the private rights of copyright owners and the public's widely asserted right of access to information. Accordingly, a watch must be kept on the pot as a whole, not on just the boil of individual bubbles. For as time goes on, it will become increasingly clear, I am sure, that the preservation of the copyright principle is indeed the sine qua non of our industry—the very key to survival.

It can be expected, of course, that publishers will always be accused of self-interest when they defend the essentiality of strict copyright protection, and this must be admitted as the truth. But at the same time it can be argued that they are thereby serving the public interest as well, to say nothing of the individual interests of authors, artists, composers, and performers of creative works. It seems to me that book publishers have not enough emphasized the societal point of view in arguing the case for strict protection. This failure has, I believe, contributed to the hardening of adversary positions that might have been avoided.

In any case, our industry would do well to promote recognition of several aspects of copyright protection that are often overlooked by the public.

First, it should be recognized that the basic nature of copyright under the U.S. law is extensional and propagative, not restrictive and monopolistic, as it often is claimed to be. Since copyright functions to stimulate and reward the creation, publication, and wide dissemination of original works, it actually promotes rather than restricts the flow of knowledge. Copyright protects only the "form of the embodiment" of ideas and information, so it imposes absolutely no restriction on the flow and use of the ideas and information, or on the material and intellectual values that are contained in copyrighted works. On the contrary, it is obvious that without adequate copyright protection the publication and dissemination of new works by creative and authoritative persons would be discouraged; and thus the flow of new ideas, new information, and fresh inspiration would be seriously restricted. And so, in the end, knowledge would be restricted and learning itself would be hindered.

Second, publishers should stress the fact that, contrary to popular belief, they generally support the doctrine of fair use as a valuable instrument of the public's interest—and of their own interest as well. As a practical matter, publishers (or authors who retain copyright in their works) do not want the onerous bother and expense of dealing with permission for inconsequential and harmless uses of reasonable portions of copyrighted works—of uses for such purposes as criticism, comment, news reporting, teaching, scholarship, and research. Indeed, such uses usually are welcomed as being conducive to public awareness of the referenced work. Still, publishers have not been able to establish their true position with convincing clarity: that in opposing unfair use, they have no intention of restricting fair use.

Third, more recognition should be given to the importance of copyright for the protection of the integrity of an author's work. This is a matter of importance to society as well as to the individual author, but it is something that is taken for granted by the public. Few people are aware of the liberties that can be taken legally with published works that are not copyrighted and thus are in the public domain. For example, such a work can be drastically edited and republished under the author's name so long as a brief notice "Edited by Joe Doakes" is placed somewhere on the cover or the title page of the republished work. Further, anyone can make a translation of an uncopyrighted work in any language and publish it under the author's name without any control whatever over the content or quality of the translated version. Thus, without copyright protection, these and other similar spurious things could happen to any published work. Patently, to let them happen freely would not be in the public interest.

Another area where the public-interest argument can be applied is in meeting demands for exemptions of nonprofit uses of copyrighted materials. In recent years, such demands—coming largely from the organizations of educators, librarians, and scientists—have ranged all the way from a more liberal concept of fair use to an unrestricted right to use any copyrighted work in any way for "the public benefit." Some proponents of this view have gone so far as to demand exemptions of all not-for-profit uses. Others have argued, on a collateral track, that copyright should not be allowed to deter the development of educational and information systems employing the new technology for information transfer, or to limit the effectiveness of educational and public-service television. All of these arguments and demands are made in terms of public welfare versus private, commercial interests. They have been exacerbated, of course, by the increased availability of high-speed, low-cost photocopying machines and other devices for quick and easy replication of printed materials. Thus the crowning argument is that the traditional concept of copyright is not compatible with the advancing modern technology of communications.

Against these public-interest efforts to dilute copyright protection, authors and publishers have argued not only in their own interest but also to the point that such dilution would actually work against the public interest. They clearly see that the exemptions, if granted, would destroy much of the present incentive for the creation of several important classes of books and much of the economic viability of their publication. Thus, setting aside the moral question of equity, authors and publishers have stressed the simple, practical question of monetary incentives and economic viability. They have made it clear that when it comes to authors' royalties and publishers' profits, financial damage inflicted from nonprofit sources is no less harmful than any other kind. Similarly, when it comes to already minimal markets for many specialized educational and professional books, erosion of these markets through copying for nonprofit uses is just as harmful as any other kind of erosion. Authors and publishers have been distressed to note the numbers of educators, librarians, and researchers who have closed their eyes to these practical considerations. It is indeed ironical that so many professional people continue to press for copyright exemptions that would surely lead to impoverishment of their professional literature. How can they possibly think that the public interest can thus be served?

Here I must note that the protracted hassle over the revision of the copyright law, described earlier, caused a regrettable chill in the traditional relations between publishers and librarians. Sadly, the natural affection of book publishers for libraries and librarians was seriously diminished. Some of us on the publishing side felt that many librarians—and especially the leaders of their professional associations—were callous, even cavalier, in their attitude toward the welfare of the producers of books and serial publications. Indeed, we saw clear evidence of the librarians' overriding concern for their own convenience and for the facility of service to their patrons. In short, they displayed strong favor for the user, but little regard for the producer, of the publications that are their stock-in-trade. Understandably, this display of heavy bias stung some of us who had worked for many years in behalf of libraries and librarians. It must be admitted, of course, that there were many opportunities on each side for misunderstandings of feelings and motives. Still the rift occurred, and it will require much mending before librarians and publishers are again cuddly bedfellows.

An unfortunate misunderstanding has recently occurred on still another aspect of copyright protection. Certain librarians and academicians have somehow generated the idea that authors' rights are being diminished or preempted by an increasing insistence by publishers that copyrights be held in the name of the publishing firm. No one seems to know where or how this fiction got started, but both authors and publishers know that the holding of a copyright is a technical matter that cannot in any way adversely affect an author's interest in his book. There is no statistical information on the subject, but my personal observation is that there has been little or no change over the past 40 years in the frequency of copyright holdings by publishers. In any case, the question is moot, because, patently, the charge that authors' rights have been diminished is without substance.

As a matter of fact, most authors have always preferred to have their works copyrighted in their publishers' names. When the publishing house registers and holds a copyright, it acts as surrogate of the author's interests, and it is bound by contract to protect those interests in the author's behalf. Naturally, this obligation relieves the author of feeling responsibility for detecting and prosecuting cases of infringement or of other misuses. Besides, several other practical considerations are usually involved: The possibility of infringement is reduced when the copyright is owned by a publisher who is ready and able to prosecute an offender; the author is relieved of responsibility for dealing with requests for copying and reprinting rights, which, as noted earlier, can be quite burdensome; and the publisher takes care of proper copyright registration of original and revised and translated editions. Further, ownership of a copyright by the publisher can, in many cases, simplify the administration of an author's estate. Thus, on the whole, the author usually has much to gain and nothing to lose by allowing the publisher to hold the copyright. Certainly, the author loses no material advantage either before or after publication because rights are disposed by the terms of the publishing contract, not by the copyright. However, the prudent author who allows the publisher to hold copyright in a work should always be sure that the contract provides that the copyright shall not be assigned to another party without the author's formal consent, or that in case the book is not kept in print or the publisher goes into bankruptcy or otherwise stops business, the copyright shall unconditionally revert to the author or the heirs of the author.

On the whole, copyright ownership is a technical arrangement that should have no influence on the balance between the author's and the publisher's interests. Hence the idea that authors' rights are being increasingly eroded by publishers is no more than a conjuring up of an evil that does not exist in the practical world of book publishing. In fact, in almost all matters of copyright protection, the interests of authors and of publishers are fundamentally identical.

15

Exploiting
Foreign Markets

If publishing for home markets tests a publisher's mettle and competence, a much harder test comes with publishing for international markets. Here the path is stony and hazardous, yet it is an exciting one to travel, and the successful traveler can find much satisfaction along the way. But the hard path has daunted many U.S. publishers, and there is, to be sure, ample justification for this caution.

In most foreign countries, markets for American books are thin, sales and distribution costs are high, and purchasing power is low. (The Western European countries, the British Commonwealth nations, and Japan are, of course, exceptions.) Further, the terms and risks of customer credit are costly, which is to say that, compared with domestic experience, collections take far longer and defaults are far more frequent. Moreover, in many countries there is always the difficult problem of arranging adequate allowance of hard-currency exchange for dollar payments. And far too often, alas, there is the ever-present problem of dealing with petty local excises and with the unmentionable private emoluments that are demanded of any foreigner who wants to get business done with reasonable dispatch. Finally, in certain countries—including our closest neighbors, Canada and Mexico—there is the delicate problem of dealing with insidious attitudes of chauvinistic nationalism that are hostile to any "intrusive control" of their cultural, educational, or news media by U.S. publishers. Under all these adverse conditions, the U.S. publisher has to work twice as hard to make a satisfactory direct profit on export sales. And this seems to be why most firms have been content with their exploitation of large and ready and familiar home markets. In fact, the comparative lushness of our domestic markets was the key factor that kept American publishers from going after foreign markets in the first half of this century. European publishers were, of course, thankful for this preoccupation, and especially so were the British, who were exceedingly jealous and protective of their so-called Empire markets.

But in more recent years a number of U.S. publishers have developed wide international interests and have worked hard to increase both export sales and overseas publishing. Indeed, a few have become world leaders in both areas. But for the industry as a whole, international sales are still of minor importance in both volume and profitability. Statistical records of the value of exports are incomplete and flawed, but experts estimate it to be about 6–7% of the total annual sales of the industry. (By comparison British publishers export almost 50% of their annual production; the proportions for other Western European countries are Spain 60%, France 17%, West Germany 15%.) Nevertheless, export sales of U.S. books are quite important in certain subject areas of publishing, notably in science, technology, medicine, business practice, and industrial management. Publishers who specialize in one or more of these areas can export as much as 20% or 30% of their product. Indeed, an authoritative treatise in any one of them often sells as many copies abroad as at home.

For publishers of specialized books the unfavorable conditions that depress profits on export sales are mitigated by an advantage that indirectly adds to profits on home sales. This is the additional profit that results from larger printings at lower unit costs—

larger printings that are made possible by the addition of export sales to ordinarily limited domestic sales. To illustrate: If the publisher of a specialized treatise in science or technology can print, say, 2,000 copies for export sale in addition to 3,000 copies for domestic sale, there is a sharp reduction in the per-copy production cost and thus a substantial increase in the margin for profit on domestic sales. The result is a hidden profit, but it is nonetheless real, and it serves as an incentive to keep the specialized publisher hustling for export sales. Indeed, many monographic works now produced in the United States could not be published for domestic markets alone. Only the total international market—the combination of domestic and foreign sales—is sufficient to sustain the costs of publishing the majority of such works in our country today.

Now, it would be a grievous mistake to limit any discussion of international publishing to the foregoing material considerations—to the pluses and minuses of immediate business concern. This is because the true-blue book publisher is bound to find many nonmaterial incentives and satisfactions in being a part of the world scene, and especially of the developing-nations side of the scene. U.S. publishers in their quest for export sales around the world soon observe that their books can serve as powerful forces in national development and in international relations. Let us examine a few of the uses and values of books in this context.

First, our books serve a basic role in keeping English as the lingua franca of most of the world. It would be difficult to exaggerate the importance of having English as the international language of education, science, industry, and commerce, or to exaggerate the power of books in keeping it as such. There is far too little public recognition of this fundamental value of our books in world affairs.

Second, books serve as vehicles for international understanding of political, social, and cultural ideas and institutions. It is no exaggeration to say that next to people, books are the best ambassadors of international enlightenment and good will. This theme deserves a bit of elaboration.

In the area of political knowledge and motivation, U.S. book publishers are happy to note that, matching their export sales with the political graph in each of the 80 or 90 countries where American books are sold, we can observe that American books and tyranny appear to live together in inverse proportion.

In most countries of the world, students are the revolutionaries of today and the leaders of tomorrow. As events of the recent past have proved in several countries, the political power of the student can be ignored by a government only at its own peril. American books abroad—and especially American textbooks—are thus directed to the hands of men and women who are vital both to the future of their countries and to the future of relations between their countries and ours. Many years ago Franklin D. Roosevelt said, "Books are bullets in the battle for men's minds."

In the area of international cultural understanding, the book is, again, both basic and powerful. This is an obvious fact, but the need abroad for more knowledge and appreciation of the cultural achievements of America is not so obvious as it should be to many U.S. citizens. Our books serve not only as direct evidence of our literary achievement but also as reflectors of our achievements in all the other arts. We should not underestimate the critical nature of this particular battlefield of international politics.

Next, it can be noted that books serve all countries as basic tools for education and training—or to use the internationally hackneyed catch-phrase, for "the development of human resources." In UNESCO councils, and indeed in almost all the capital cities of the world, one continually hears much talk about the urgent and universal need for greater development of human resources—which means, in more simple and conventional language, the need for more and better education and training. Naturally, all this worldwide urge to both national and international action for more and better education and training is very heartening to book publishers everywhere, but it is especially heartening to American publishers. This is because most of the developing nations of the world have looked first to us to supply their needs for textbooks for college and graduate school courses, and they have also looked to us for help in producing their own indigenous texts for elementary and secondary schools. A number of educational publishers have responded—not without some self-interest, of course—as helpfully as possible. But everywhere we have seen appalling gaps between the needs of developing countries and the actual local market demands that can be generated for textbooks and other learning materials. In short, we have everywhere experienced the frustration of trying to fill bottomless pits of educational needs. More will be said about this in a later chapter.

Finally, books serve in a similar way as a basic guide in the development of national economic resources and in the stimulation of international trade. Everyone recognizes the essentiality of books—of operating manuals, of technical handbooks, of how-to-do-it guides, of professional treatises—in the improvement of agriculture, commerce, and industry. But only book publishers have realistically faced the problem of supplying such books in adequate quantity to the developing nations. And here again all such nations are looking to the United States to supply their needs. They want our editions in English at the higher levels of science and technology, and they also want translations and adaptations of our books at the vocational levels. They want lots and lots of both kinds, and they need them now, this year, not next year or five years from now.

Obviously, the emerging nations are prepared to import our ideas, our methods, and our technology along with our books. Thus do books serve in the vanguard of international trade. And thus do they serve in a correlative way as pioneers and conditioners of emerging new markets for U.S. materials, designs, products, and services. The British understood this well when many years ago they coined the slogan "Trade Follows the Book." And today U.S. publishers know that the country that ensures that its books are supplied to the emerging nations is forging strong two-way ties in a developing world economy.

With due regard for all the benefits and challenges that are involved, a small number of U.S. publishers have worked hard, very hard, at book exporting in the post–World War II years. We have tried to make the most of what appear to be fortunate opportunities for our books and our authors around the world. But every Eden has its serpent, and we have constantly found a two-headed monster in most of our gardens of opportunity abroad. This monster's first head, as noted earlier, is what we call high cost, while our would-be customers abroad call it high price. The second head is hard currency—the lack of available convertible currency. Without this monster, the business of exporting American books would be like finding pie in the sky; with it the going is quite rough. And, lamentably, the situation in most areas of the world is getting worse, not better. Obviously, what publishers need is a Saint George, or a troop of Saint Georges, to help us cope with the two-headed monster, for certainly the U.S. book industry alone and unassisted cannot hope to do what needs to be done. What is more, we need help the most in those countries of the world where books are indeed serving as bullets in the battle for people's minds.

Now, just where could the book industry hope to find a helpful Saint George? Well, considering the importance of books in supporting U.S. foreign policy objectives, one would think that the U.S. government would assist book export efforts aimed at all the critical "third-world" nations that are important to our country. Strangely enough, our government has given these efforts scant encouragement, much less any substantial and sustained material assistance. Traditionally, AID (U.S. Agency for International Development) has been preoccupied with the development of material resources (agriculture, industry, energy, transportation, etc.) and the USIA (United States Information Agency) has concentrated, unwisely I think, on thinly disguised propaganda programs. Regrettably, the propaganda overtone of all USIA activities has harmed most of the few library and education programs which that agency has sponsored overseas. And, strangely, the USIA bureaucrats in charge of developing-country education programs have consistently been unable to cut through their maze of educational theory and practice to the material fact that the availability of adequate supplies of textbooks and other teaching materials is the sine qua non of any successful education program anywhere in the world.

All this indifference and ineptness of federal officials has, of course, disheartened many U.S. publishers who think they should have some effective governmental support of their efforts to increase the supplies of textbooks in the developing countries where teaching materials are as much needed as modern educational ideas and model curricula. But, regrettably, the book industry has failed to muster enough interest and persuasion to make even a slight dent on bureaucratic attitudes in Washington.

What is needed by American book publishers—and by all other exporters of educational and informational products—is a quasi-governmental promotional organization similar to the British Council. That organization, though modest in size and cost, serves very effectively in helping United Kingdom exporters to penetrate foreign markets that are politically or culturally sensitive to outside "imperialistic" intrusion. It is far more effective than the USIA for the simple reason that, though funded largely by government grants, it is isolated from direct governmental identity and influence. Its offices and services in foreign countries are operated quietly and without observable connections with British embassies or consular offices. Thus they are shielded from the kinds of ideological and political conflict that have so often disrupted our USIA programs. In a number of countries USIA libraries have been ravaged or burned to the ground, but I have never heard of a British Council's office anywhere being molested by hostile agitators. It is, I suppose, a reflection of the difference between silk-glove and hard-fist styles of diplomacy. Be that as it may, the British Council promotional efforts seem to reap goodwill everywhere, while our USIA programs far too often seem to attract resentment and brickbats.

It is a great pity that, to date, all efforts to interest possibly responsive government officials in the operating facade and style of the British Council have failed. But it must be said that the U.S. book industry has not yet backed a cogent and sustained effort to convince such officials that we could copy the British example to our own great benefit. One can only hope that our internationally minded publishers will look upon this as an important piece of unfinished business in Washington. And, as indicated in a later chapter, it appears that still another effort will soon be made to organize an international book development center that will serve both book-industry and governmental interests all over the world.

16

International Publishing Becomes Multinational Publishing

As noted earlier, it was not until the end of World War II that U.S. publishers seriously started to exploit international book markets. During the war years, the British and German publishers were cut off from their export markets, and much of the neutral market demand shifted to the United States. Thus, for the first time, U.S. publishers generally became aware that several kinds of their books could be sold abroad profitably. A number of us roused ourselves and rushed into export marketing, some boldly, others tentatively.

With the recovery of the book industries of Great Britain and Germany after the war, and with several French firms coming on more strongly in the international scene, export selling on a worldwide scale soon became a hard-fought contest among the leading four countries. Meanwhile, the Spanish publishers had stepped up their output and aggressively increased their sales to

Latin America, which soon would account for 70 percent of their total exports. In those postwar recovery years, U.S. publishers soon learned something about the astuteness and toughness of their European competitors in the growing world markets.

In the 1950s there occurred two other kinds of growth in international publishing, the one a quick mushrooming, the other a budding that would in time open into full flower.

The first was the production of co-editions of illustrated books in several languages by *ad hoc* international consortiums of publishers. This kind of publishing was started with great success for books on the fine arts. It soon spread to books on other subjects that also need many illustrations—architecture, archaeology, travel, geography, etc. Later, many heavily illustrated dictionaries and encyclopedias were produced in the same way but with less economic advantage. In time the genre was to include books on any subject where illustrations were essential and of equal importance with the text matter. Thus came into being the "coffee-table" book, denigrated by book reviewers but loved by publishers, booksellers, and millions of buyers. Copious color illustrations were, of course, the touchstone of success; the practice of printing all the color plates for several different language editions resulted in prices that were acceptable to general book buyers in all affluent countries of the world. This advent of the coffee-table book had a large and beneficial impact on bookselling in all the major countries involved in its production and in some book-importing countries as well.

Still it must be observed that, strictly speaking, this coproduction of multinational editions is not true international publishing. To begin with, the best specimen of this genre is a book on a universal subject, first planned and written for a particular national market. The co-editions are, in fact, no more than several translations printed simultaneously, each for a national or a national-language market. And even the national-language market concept does not hold for the English-language edition; it is usually split between a British and an American publisher. (In some cases two English-language editions are produced—one in English English, the other in American English.) Indeed, the idea of international sales runs contrary to the usual arrangement for coproduction of multinational editions because the arrangement is explicitly designed to divide the world into national or national-language market segments. In short, the arrangement is one for all in the production phase, but every one for oneself, and unto oneself, in the marketing phase. Thus, this kind of activity can be labeled more properly as multinational *production* rather than international *publishing*.

The second kind of growth also occurred with the book industry's recovery from the ravages of World War II. This was the flowering of an earlier budding—a flowering that became, in time, true international publishing. It started with the establishment of branch offices overseas by a number of the larger European publishers—British, French, and Spanish—and by a few American houses. These branch offices functioned in dual capacity as export sales agencies and as publishers for the countries or regions of their location. Such a sales agency-*cum*-publisher would issue a few indigenous titles, but mostly it produced translations or same-language editions adapted to local needs. Most of the local publishing was of tertiary level textbooks, but a literary title would sweeten the list now and then. In any case, this was predominately a one-way kind of international publishing by the mother house, and in several instances a brood of international branch operations came, in time, to be substantial contributors to the mother's prosperity. Indeed, in a few instances—notably Longmans and Oxford University Press in England, Hachette in France, and Aguilar and Salvat in Spain—the brood produced an important part of the mother's total publishing income and profit.

Through the 1950s and the 1960s, these dual-purpose branch offices grew in size and proliferated in number. Many of them turned into locally incorporated subsidiary companies, some of which were to dominate the local publishing scene. Some remained wholly owned subsidiaries; others invited local participation in ownership and management. Some became active exporters of their indigenous lists, selling both to the mother company and to open markets around the world. Thus there came into being the one-firm multinational complex engaged in what truly was international publishing.

Also in the 1960s, a number of large European and American houses further expanded their international operations by establishing new jointly owned subsidiaries or by acquiring whole or part ownership in established firms of other countries. This kind of expansion, capping what had gone before, produced combines that are truly multinational both in character and in operational concept. Indeed, through this growth process, certain large firms are gradually being denationalized. Each of them has many home markets and many export markets. In a sense all their markets are "overseas," and all are served by books from several countries. This is international publishing in its purest sense, and perhaps the time has come to call it by its right name, multinational publishing.

The largest of the multinational publishers are Hachette, based in France; Bertelsmann and Georg Von Holtzbrinck, based in Germany; and Doubleday, Time-Life, Prentice-Hall, and McGraw-Hill, all based in the United States. (This list excludes several very large specialized publishers of encyclopedias and reference books and of bibles and other books on religion, all of which have very large multinational sales.) In order to give a sense of how such a company operates in the world scene, I shall describe the one I know best.

The McGraw-Hill International Book Company has grown in the past three decades through all the developmental stages described above. Currently, it comprises an export department in the United States, eleven wholly owned foreign subsidiaries, two partly owned foreign subsidiaries, two minority-interest holdings in other countries, and two import sales offices. Thus, multinational operations of various kinds are carried on in seventeen countries.

The wholly owned companies are in England, Germany, Spain, South Africa, Australia, New Zealand, Mexico, Colombia, Panama, Portugal, and Brazil. The partly owned subsidiaries are in Canada and Japan. The minority-interest holdings are in Switzerland and India. The import sales offices are in France and Singapore.

English-language books of local origin are published in seven countries; Spanish-language books in three countries; Portugese books in two countries; and German, French, Afrikaans, Arabic, Hindi, and Japanese each in one country.

Of the dollar value of current overseas sales of McGraw-Hill books, about 57 percent is derived from titles published or reprinted outside the United States. If the present trend continues, that proportion will be about 75 to 80 percent a decade hence. Yet, at the same time, it is expected that direct export sales from the United States will steadily increase in absolute volume.

This worldwide country/language complex has produced many synergies, a few of which may have large significance for the future. Each McGraw-Hill subsidiary in an English-language country concentrates on publishing for its home market, but each also produces textbooks and professional and reference books that can be sold by the other subsidiary companies. Thus each feeds, and feeds upon, the others. For example, of the annual sales of the books published by the British subsidiary, about 35 percent goes to the parent U.S. company and to the "sister" companies in Canada, Australia, New Zealand, South Africa, India, and Japan. Also, McGraw-Hill's well-established French-language publishing program in Montreal exports a good part of its production to the company's import-sales office in Paris.

In addition to the subsidiaries and partnerships just described, McGraw-Hill has two production centers abroad that operate solely as editorial and production centers, which is to say that they sell their editions only and wholly to McGraw-Hill companies or to non-English-language publishers on a contracted, coproduction basis.

The older of the two centers is the Co-Publishing Division, located at Lucerne, Switzerland. This division generates, edits, designs, and prints (in large runs of 50,000 to 150,000 copies) heavily illustrated books produced as joint ventures with other leading European publishers. All these books are printed with one large and economical run of color plates and with texts in five to eight different languages—a very difficult and exacting job in each case!

The newer venture, the Center for Advanced Publishing, is located at Dusseldorf, Germany. It produces high-level scientific and technical monographs (English-language only) for academic and research professionals throughout the world. Their editions are marketed solely through the units of the McGraw-Hill multinational complex. Many of them are translations of excellent but little-known French, German, Scandinavian, and Russian books.

To complete the picture it should be noted that, along with the expansion of multinational publishing on its own, McGraw-Hill continues to encourage and promote translations of its books by other publishers in all parts of the world. In recent years, translation rights have been licensed at the rate of about 400 titles per year, a substantial increase over the rate of earlier years. It is significant to observe that Japanese has recently rivaled Spanish as the leading language for translation contracts, while Portugese, Italian, German, and French follow in this traditional order. Further down the line, but of growing importance to the firm and its authors, are Marathi, Tamil, Gujarati, Sinhala, and Swahili. It appears, in fact, that translations into some of the "exotic" languages of Asia and Africa will, in time, become as important as certain more familiar European languages.

So goes the trend in international publishing. Where it will end nobody knows. But for some major U.S. publishers it will end, I suppose, in the optimum situation—a situation in which each will have a dual-purpose company in every major country or market area of the world, and in which direct export from the "home" location will be a thing of the past. Under this ideal and ultimate concept, with multinational publishing and international selling combined in one worldwide complex, every major firm will come to think of the world as being its oyster.

Looking ahead with this developmental strategy in mind, one can be sure of three things. First, the race will be for the strong and the bold; when more large firms move into multinational operations, the competition will become ever rougher and tougher. Second, the rewards for success will be great because many now-latent book industries of the developing countries will benefit through joint ventures with resources that could never be mustered locally. On the other hand, one can be rather sure that many publishers of all countries will continue to disparage the development of multinational enterprises of the size and resources and power that have been here described. To repeat, ours is supposed to be a genteel occupation in which one should stay at home and cultivate the garden in quiet intellection and ease. To my way of thinking, this idea of the proper book publisher lost its validity throughout the Western world many years ago.

As a footnote to this disquisition, it should be observed that publishers who take to the hard roads to foreign markets will surely find their business enterprises expanded in ways that are difficult but exciting, and they are also likely to find their personal horizons expanded in ways that are rewarding and gratifying. They will see many interesting and exotic corners of the world that otherwise they might never have ventured to visit. This in itself can be a rich personal reward. "Roam abroad in the world," said an ancient Persian poet, "and take thy fill of it before the day shall come when thou must quit it for good." Many U.S. publishers, including myself, have found that roaming abroad has been the greatest joy of their careers.

17

Helping Indigenous Publishing in Needy Countries

More deserves to be said here about the U.S. book publishers' adjunctive interest in helping with the special problems of book development in the underprivileged areas of the world. For the past quarter century, a compound motivation has prompted a number of us to do what we reasonably could do with credibility in this kind of international activity. The first part of the motivation is the humane desire to promote literacy everywhere; the second part is our more selfish and quite speculative long-range interest in creating future markets for our own books. (We should, of course, no more take credit for the one than apologize for the other.) In any case, all of us who are active in this area think we see quite clearly that the key to the creation of these new markets will be the promotion of an indigenous publishing program that will meet the peculiar needs—and especially the particular educational needs—of each developing country.

But there is much more to the development of indigenous publishing than the availability of suitable facilities and materials and capital for the printing of books. Some years ago, a friend of mine went to the heart of the matter by remarking wryly: "Of one thing I'm at last firmly convinced: You can't fill book gaps with books." As an officer of a large international organization, he had had opportunities to observe a number of book-development programs in several parts of the world over a 20-year period. Hearing his enigmatic remark, I had expected my friend to go on and say that he had found the book gaps of the world to be so wide and so deep as to preclude any hope that enough books ever could be produced to fill them. But this simple cliché was not the burden of his thought.

What the remark meant, he explained, was that in his observation far too many book-development programs had failed because they had concentrated on production and neglected distribution and utilization. In too many cases, after thousands of desperately needed books had been produced, it was discovered that far too many copies were left sitting in warehouses—that there were no suitable mechanisms or facilities for effective movement of the books into the gaps. Nor were the gaps adequately prepared to receive the books and to make effective use of them. What my friend really meant, of course, was that book gaps cannot be filled by books *alone*—that the supply of books, no matter how plentiful, will not fill a country's need unless adequate marketing mechanisms and sufficient distribution channels have been provided, and unless rewarding use of the books is assured in the end.

My friend's astute observation is significant on two counts: First, it puts the problem of indigenous publishing into a properly balanced economic perspective; second, it suggests that publishers everywhere have the responsibility to remind the planners and movers of book-development programs that there is much more to successful publishing than the mere production of needed books in the largest quantities that can be afforded. Indeed, publishers everywhere have the obligation to clarify for all concerned the true nature of book gaps in almost all developing countries. In thinking about these gaps and in attempting to deal with them, it is important to make a clear distinction between the real *need* and the *effective demand* for books. To the intelligent but uninformed outsider (and, indeed, to some insiders who should know better), the book gap has seemed to be simply a shortage of books. This conclusion too often has led to narrowly planned aid programs designed only to increase the quantity of books in print—programs such as the ones my friend was sighing over. Most of these programs have failed, or are failing, because in fact the gap is between the effective *market demand* and the real *need*. To put it another way, the created market demand has come nowhere near matching the national need. In a good number of countries that have serious books gaps, the book industry has the capacity to produce very nearly as many books as are needed. In those countries the real problem is to stimulate the consumers— governmental, institutional, and private—to want and to use more books and to allocate sufficient financial resources to the purchase of books to create effective market demands. This developmental strategy is possible only through broadly based programs and methods that are not often enough associated with mere gap-filling book production. All publishers know that editing skills, printing facilities, and production materials are of little value if supporting markets for the published product are not readily accessible and favorably conditioned. This basic economic fact must be clearly understood as well by our book-minded friends and colleagues in education, government, international organizations, and private philanthropy. (It was clearly understood by Paul Hoffman, who stated on his retirement from a long career of distinguished service in international aid at the United Nations: "One illusion is that you can industrialize a country by building factories. You don't. You industrialize it by building markets.")

Now, how does a developing nation create an effective market demand for books? How does it sustain the demand at a level that will support a viable book industry? In short, how does it go about the task of reducing the gap between the often seemingly *limitless* national need for books and the *limited* actual market for them?

In seeking the answers to these questions, one must look first to the market for educational books, which nearly everywhere is not only the largest but also the most profitable of all for indigenous book publishers. Hence the development of this market is of primary importance in the development of a book industry that will adequately serve a nation's needs. In order to develop an effective market demand, the educational system must, of course, be organized to encourage the use of books as basic tools of instruction and to instill lifetime reading habits in students. Further, as noted earlier, sufficient financial resources must be allocated for the purchase of books for at least minimal use by *all* students, not just those of well-to-do families. This means that the book component must be planned and built in as a carefully integrated part of the total educational system. All too often this is not done. All too often books are presumed to be a basic educational necessity, yet unlike other basics their purchase is not adequately provided for.

It is hard to explain this neglect because even in countries where educational books are plentifully provided, their cost is only a small fraction of the total cost of the education system. In the United States, for example, the expenditure for books and other printed educational materials, including school and college library purchases, has been less than 2 percent of the total expenditures on education for recent years. The smallness of this fraction surprises many people both at home and abroad. They find it hard to believe. I venture to say, however, that if the facts were known, the fraction would be even smaller in most other industrially developed countries. Hence, it seems that publishers everywhere should emphasize the fact that in the economy of education the cost of books is actually a low factor—very low, certainly, in relation to the high educative value of books. The point needs to be hammered home in those developing countries where almost no public money is provided for educational books.

In final reference to the economic importance of the educational book markets in developing countries, I must make an observation that is admittedly both doctrinaire and debatable. It has to do with the nationalization of textbook production in certain of these countries. Plainly, any substantial engagement of a government as publisher is bound to have a repressive influence on the development of a private-enterprise book industry. As noted above, in almost all developed countries the production of educational books is the mainstay of the publishing industry. It follows, then, that wherever this economically important area is preempted by the government, it will be very difficult for private industry to service adequately the nation's need for other kinds of essential books.

In making this statement, I recognize the fact that governmental production is the only way in which even minimal needs for textbooks can be met at present in certain developing countries. But even in such cases, the validity of my point can be argued as an important consideration in a nation's long-range developmental plan.

Now, what other factors are especially critical in developing countries? First, in logical order, comes the economy of manufacture. Here it is of primary importance to note that the scarcity of materials usually is more critical than that of machinery or skilled labor. Paper, inks, and binding materials usually are in short supply and have to be heavily imported by developing countries. This involves problems of cost and foreign-currency exchange, which are painfully familiar everywhere. Moreover, many nations that desperately need low-priced books have imposed substantial import duties on book-manufacturing materials, yet have allowed duty-free import of manufactured books. Clearly, this senseless behavior not only handicaps indigenous publishing and printing; it also broadly hinders educational and economic development. This practice has been widely protested, but alas, in most underdeveloped countries, ministers of finance never listen to ministers of education or even to ministers of information.

Next comes the economy of distribution, about which one can only remark the obvious: No book publishing industry anywhere can adequately serve a nation's needs without the support of a sound and efficient network of competent wholesalers and retailers. Yet in most developing countries little attention is given—even by publishers—to the essentiality of such a distribution system. Far too often publishers and booksellers alike are guilty of irregular trading practices that create havoc in the marketplace—practices that cause hostility and distrust where harmony and mutual help should be the rule. Disrupted and uneconomic distribution is hurtful, obviously, to the public interest as well as to the book industry. It seems, then, that publishers everywhere (with only a few countries excepted) have a special obligation to work much harder at the elimination of un-fair, disruptive, and hurtful trade practices.

Next, and closely related to distribution, comes the economy of transport. This is far more important to the book industry than the casual observer might think. Indeed, the foregoing proposi-tion can be extended by saying that no book-distribution system anywhere can function well without fast, safe, and low-cost ship-ping facilities. Governments that want more books at lower costs made readily available to the total population must help with this problem by providing preferred postal rates and subsidized freightage; also, by protecting against pilferage and other dis-honest and unlawful occurrences in transport. In many a country the lack of economic and dependable transport has by itself con-fined book markets to one or two large metropolitan centers. What a pity!

Finally comes the crowning financial problem of working capi-tal—which always is especially acute, of course, in countries where owned capital is scarce and borrowed capital is hard to come by, even at the highest rates of interest. Now, everywhere in the world—even in the most affluent countries—most book publishers have to go to their bankers at least once or twice a year. Often it is a year-round, never-ending visit. And, alas, al-most everywhere bankers look upon publishing loans with eyes that are colder than usual, and publishers have to pay higher than usual interest rates. Unfortunately, in most countries of the world, book publishing is not looked upon as a prime business risk. In certain developing countries, publishers pay rates as high as 20 to 40 percent on fully secured short-term commercial loans.

The chief cause of this financial stress is, naturally, the slow-ness in turnover of the publisher's working capital. Under even the most favorable conditions, prepublication investments (largely editorial expense) turn over about once in two years, in-ventory investments about once a year, and receivables about four times a year. (In the United States the major item, in-ventories, presently turns over 1.3 times per year; in the major European countries the rate is considerably lower.) Borrowing capital to finance this kind of business operation puts a squeeze on publishers throughout the world. Naturally, the squeeze is especially hurtful in developing countries, where it has several grievous effects, some of which are readily observable, some not.

First, the squeeze causes short-run printings, which result, of course, in higher unit costs and higher consumer prices. Too often books must be produced and priced for quick get-out on one printing only, and thus the price and profit benefits of low-cost second and subsequent printings are lost. And thus, also, many a good book is lost to continuing public use.

Second, in the interest of time/money savings, many books are sent to press before they are ready. Thus editorial quality is sacrificed. This is especially lamentable in the production of textbooks and professional books.

Third, funds for announcement and promotion expense following publication are often curtailed. This is harmful to desired public awareness and to sales as well.

Fourth, the need to turn slow-moving inventory into cash often prompts unsound business practices, such as special discounts and dumping in bargain markets, which are demoralizing to the book trade as a whole.

Fifth, publishers are motivated to fill their lists with "quickie" sensational books and to forego more solid and more badly needed books that require larger and longer-term capital investment.

In view of all these harmful consequences of high-cost working capital, it seems that all governments of developing countries and all interested international organizations and public-interest foundations must pay much more attention to the financial need of indigenous book publishing enterprises. A curing of this basic economic debility would quickly cure many of the related secondary ailments that usually receive much more attention.

Anyone who wants more detailed information on the economic stringencies of indigenous publishing in needy countries should read a UNESCO report that was completed in 1976 by Datus C. Smith, Jr., under the auspices of Franklin Book Programs, Inc., and published in 1977.[1] This report gives details of the publishing costs of sampled publishers in four regions of the world: Asia, Latin America, Middle East, and Africa. For each, the elements of manufacturing and editorial costs are broken down, and general overhead and distribution costs are estimated as carefully as possible. Questions of national languages, of government publishing, and of the possibilities of inter-country co-publishing are discussed knowledgeably and frankly.

Mr. Smith's study has special value in one particular: It demolishes the almost universally believed fiction that the cost of translation rights for developed countries' books has placed a heavy burden on the publishers of developing countries. The study discovered the fact that the average cost of translation rights for all regions were only 6.2 percent of the list prices of the translated editions. Since publishers customarily pay only half of the translation fee in advance of publication, this single element of cost usually is a little over 3 percent of the list price. In comparison, the two major elements of cost in relation to list price are: manufacturing, 30.5 percent, and out-of-pocket overhead, 12.5 percent. It seems, then, that the familiar claim of high translation fees as being the principal restraint on the production of more and cheaper books in needy countries has lost its credibility—even in UNESCO-sponsored book development conferences, where the claim has been so often accepted at face value.[2]

More must be said here about the prominent role of Franklin Book Programs, Inc., in assisting indigenous publishing in needy countries. Franklin was established in 1952 as a not-for-profit organization governed by a board of directors comprised of leading publishers, educators, public officials, and corporation executives. Its efforts have been supported by governments (U.S. and others), foundations, universities, corporations, and many dedicated individuals. Its program objectives have been: "(1) To increase local capabilities through technical assistance and training in the planning, production, and dissemination of educational materials at all levels of developing societies; (2) To increase international exchange of knowledge through translation and copyright services, stimulation of international trade, conferences, and exhibits; (3) To strengthen marketing and distribution of locally produced and imported educational materials; (4) To develop the reading habit through reading-reinforcement materials; library development and utilization particularly for children; assistance to literacy campaigns."[3]

With headquarters in New York, Franklin has at one time or another had developmental programs in Cairo, Beirut, Bagdad, Tehran, Tabriz, Lahore, Dacca, Kuala Lumpur, Kathmandu, Jakarta, Kabul, Lagos, and Manila. For one reason or another, all the overseas offices have been closed or spun off as independent local organizations, usually because Franklin's mission in each particular country had been accomplished.

Starting initially at Cairo, and operating largely with start-up funds provided by the USIA, Franklin assisted in the production of more than 400 translated Arabic editions of U.S. books within its first ten years. It acquired translation rights from U.S. publishers for nominal fees; financed high-quality translations; and then assigned translated titles to competent local publishers who produced the books on a commercial basis, with a reimbursing royalty paid to Franklin in local currency. This pattern of operations was soon extended to other countries, and within the initial decade some 700 other translated editions were published in the Farsi, Urdu, Bengali, Malay, Indonesian, and Pushtu languages.

From these starting programs, Franklin branched out by financing and overseeing the production of new, modern encyclopedias in the Arabic, Farsi, Bengali, Urdu, and Indonesian languages. In addition, it assisted in the indigenous production of textbooks, school magazines and audiovisual materials, technical pamphlets, and higher-level professional books and journals. In recent years, the planning and administration of local training programs became a major activity, sponsored usually by developing-country governments.

In its first quarter century of operations, more than 3,000 titles were translated and produced through Franklin. For all its programs, more than $100 million was expended in various currencies. About $20 million of this came from U.S. sources, and only $600,000 was contributed in cash by the U.S. book industry. The rest came from earned income and government contracts in foreign countries. (Actually, the U.S. book industry has an even cash balance with Franklin; our publishers have received a total of about $600,000 in rights and royalty payments.)

In spite of this outstanding record of success, Franklin Book Programs had to struggle for its existence in the 1970s. Anyone who is not thoroughly familiar with Franklin's history might well ask how this could happen. There are several reasons why it did happen, some of them sound, others false or factious.

First, as noted earlier, Franklin fulfilled its original mission in several countries by producing as many translated editions as national or area markets could absorb.

Second, there were, inevitably, a few cases of incompetent, even dishonest, management of field offices. Naturally, they caused a considerable amount of both local and home-office disaffection.

Third, in Iran and Afghanistan, Franklin's activity assisted government-directed monopolies of textbook production, including the design and operation of three new and modern printing plants. This blocking of private-enterprise publishing disquieted a good number of U.S. publishers who had supported Franklin's efforts in other countries.

Fourth, Franklin forfeited much of its U.S. government support by refusing to limit its sponsorship to books that were in line with U.S. foreign policy objectives as interpreted by AID and USIA program officers. Hassling over this point of principle went on for many years.

Now, on balance, what can be said of Franklin's past performance and future prospect? Well, those of us who have seen both the rise and descent of Franklin's fortune—who have shared its troubles at home and observed its successes abroad—are uneasy about its position. We know that Franklin has well served the interests of our industry and our government; that it has served even better the interests of many book-hungry countries around the world, where it still enjoys much confidence and high reputation. But we also know that it has lost much of the appeal of its original mission; that, consequently, it must be phased out unless new and more attractive programs can soon be found. Still, we should not give up hope that the internationally minded leaders of our industry will not abandon their efforts to save the Franklin concept—if not as an institution, then as an operating unit in a larger and broader organization for the worldwide promotion of U.S. books. Certainly, such a well-established and reputable institution as Franklin should not be allowed to sink completely out of sight.

As noted at the outset, an increasing number of American publishers have devoted much time and effort to promoting book-development programs in underdeveloped countries. This has been done by participation in regional conferences (usually sponsored by UNESCO) and in national conferences sponsored by local book-development councils; also by supplying, gratis, management and expert personnel for workshops and technical training courses. The essentiality of market development has now become widely accepted in principle. However, the idea of supplying low-cost working capital for book publishing has been very hard to sell. (It is always less difficult to accept ideas—even new ones—than it is to give money.) Many countries have turned to UNESCO for assistance in establishing "Book Bank" funds (and not without unwarranted encouragement), but this has been in vain because UNESCO has not had that kind of money to spend. In recent years, the World Bank's International Finance Corporation and several regional developmental banks have evinced some real and informed interest in the problem. One can only hope that these financial organizations are at last beginning to see that every developing country is as much in need of low-cost capital for its book industry as for its hydraulic dams, its highways and railroads, its manufacturing plants—yes, even for its paper mills and printing plants.

18

The Use and Disuse of Trade Associations

Since book publishers by nature are individualists who like to think and act with independence, it is natural that they have always found it difficult to work together in a trade organization. Further, some publishers have a historically engendered fear of encountering the law through charges of restraint-of-trade activities. Others have an innate dislike or disdain of pressure-group activity of any sort; in their view lobbying or wire-pulling is not nice, even when done for good causes. Then there are, always, certain publishers who will sit in callosity on the side-lines and take freely all advantages that may come their way from the efforts of others.

These characteristic behavioral traits have made it difficult for the book industry to support a strong and widely based trade association. The difficulty is attested by the fact that five different associations were organized in the first half of the century, and only recently (after 1970) has a really powerful, industry-wide association finally emerged.

The APA (American Publishers Association) was organized in 1900. Its principal purpose was to try to stabilize book prices by eliminating price-cutting practices of department stores. The members of the association agreed to maintain "net" prices of their books by refusing to sell to dealers who cut prices or sold to retail customers at a discount. After resisting this cartellike arrangement for many months, R. H. Macy and Company brought a restraint-of-trade suit against the association—and also against the ABA (American Booksellers Association), which was cooperating with the publishers. The suit was filed at the end of 1902, but the matter was not settled until 1913, when the Supreme Court decided unanimously in favor of Macy. The decision turned on the question of whether copyright provided the proprietor of a book the right to fix its price; the Court held that copyright is not exempt from the Sherman Antitrust Act. Macy was awarded $140,000 in damages, and this penalty resulted in the dissolution of the APA. That experience dampened the spirit of trade cooperation in the book industry for many years to come.

Nevertheless, the NABP (National Association of Book Publishers) was organized in 1920. It was a relatively low-keyed organization, run conservatively by the heads of the larger trade book houses. But its leadership was soon sorely divided over a censorship issue. At the instigation of the notorious John Sumner of the New York Society for the Suppression of Vice, a Clean Books Bill had been introduced in the New York State Legislature. It was stoutly opposed by the Authors League and branded by the *New York Times* as "the worst censorship bill yet proposed." Yet the NABP, guided by its censorship committee, of which Charles Scribner was chairman, decided to take no action in opposition to the bill. This enraged Horace Liveright and several other libertarians, who thereafter took separate and private action. The bill passed the state assembly by a large margin, but Liveright, aided by New York City politician Jimmy Walker, succeeded in lobbying its defeat in the senate. Liveright then celebrated at a victory dinner where he announced his resignation from the national association and charged that two of its prominent members had actually helped to write the bill. Naturally, this hardened feelings, but the association held together and functioned in rather a pedestrian way until 1937 when it quietly succumbed to the economic ravages of the depression years.

But that demise did not halt all trade association activity. At the start of 1938 a group of publishers formed a successor organization to carry on a part of the defunct NABP program. Called the BPB (Book Publishers Bureau), its primary purpose was to continue the NABP's credit-information service. Its secondary purpose was "to watch legislation of importance to the book industry, copyright, censorship, and other similar types of bills, and report to the publishers affiliated with the Bureau." The budget for the first year was all of $25,000, of which two-thirds was allotted to the credit-information service. Actually, almost the whole amount was spent for that service, and the "legislation-watching" service was soon forgotten. But the bureau's one-man staff did manage to conduct a credit service that was of much value to the book industry for almost a decade.

It was not until 1942 that events forced another grouping of publishers to organize for their collective interests. In that year representatives of 28 textbook publishers met in New York and formed the ATPI (American Textbook Publishers Institute). The announced purpose of the new organization was not to deal with trade practices, but "to study and seek to reach a constructive solution of all problems having to do with the use of textbooks as the tools of learning." Accordingly, its activities would aim to "promote better understanding by the public of the place and the need of the textbook in American education, formulate a public relations program to increase the public service rendered by the industry, encourage and cooperate in stimulating research on textbooks and teaching problems directly affecting the use of textbooks, and assist in helping to win the war and the peace that will follow by cooperating with our national government and its agencies."

In spite of this statement of its lofty purpose and program, the institute's first order of business was a vigorous effort to enlarge the War Production Board's allocation of paper for the manufacture of textbooks. This was, to be sure, a very worthy cause; large amounts of textbooks were needed for burgeoning war-training programs, but the military departments had forgotten that paper was needed for their production. (Once at that time when I applied to a high-ranking Naval officer for assistance with a paper-quota problem, he reproachfully said, "If McGraw-Hill can't supply the books we need for our navigation courses, we shall buy them from Brentano or Random House or another dealer who can supply them.")

After the war was over, the ATPI conveniently forgot its founders' declaration of purpose and thereafter devoted almost all of its efforts to problems of book production and of trade relations that directly affected the profitability of textbook publishing. Little attention was given to problems of research or public relations, and the importance of government relations was all but completely neglected—of which more will be said later.

The effectiveness of the ATPI was viewed with feelings of envy and rivalry by many general book publishers. These feelings preordained the establishment in 1946 of the ABPC by representatives of 54 firms. Most of them were primarily trade-book houses, but some were, of course, members of the ATPI also. The announced objectives were broad in scope and considerable in number—indeed, they laid out an idealized charter for a trade association, far more than could possibly be undertaken with a meager budget and a small staff. But it must be said that, as time went on, the ABPC did far more for the benefit of the book industry generally than did the more narrowly oriented ATPI.

So for 25 years—from 1946 to 1971—the book industry struggled along with two trade associations that had an ever-increasing overlap of memberships and programs, and an ever-increasing identicalness of interest and purpose. Both associations grew slowly in size and resources, but the industry spoke with two voices and acted in separate ways that were not always consonant. This caused confusion and occasional contradictions, both within the industry and in its external relations. In time, many houses that had large interests in both textbook and general publishing became irked by the dual efforts and the necessity of supporting the separate organizations. Also, they saw that distinctions between the two kinds of publishing were being rapidly erased in the marketplaces. Thus the sentiment for amalgamation grew in force, and finally at the 1959 annual meetings of both organizations, I myself formally proposed a merger. As the result, an inevitable joint committee was appointed to consider ways and means.

Thereafter, it took ten years of niggling and hassling and infighting and strong-armed bargaining for the development and promotion of an acceptable plan of merger. As was to be expected, most of the opposition came from the "pure" houses, either purely textbook or purely trade-book publishers. It was soon seen that each side distrusted the other more than most of us had thought possible. But the joint committee persisted stoutly and nobly, and finally the amalgamated AAP was organized in 1971. At the end it appeared that the contentious opposition on each side had worn itself out, for very few members were lost in the merger. In any case, the book industry did at last manage to establish a reasonably strong industry-wide trade association to protect and promote its national interests.

If U.S. book publishers were conventionally apathetic toward their national trade associations, they were, with a very few exceptions, cold toward active participation in the IPA (International Publishers Association). In the first half of the century, that organization (an association of national trade associations of book and music publishers) operated largely as an instrument and mouthpiece of European members. However, the United States maintained a nominal membership for several years through its national association, and one or two American representatives regularly attended the biennial meetings. In the World War II years, the IPA was forced to suspend its program, but it was revived soon after the end of the war. The IPA secretariat then rashly assumed that the newly organized ABPC would carry on the U.S. membership and would also pay dues for the elapsed years. This assumption was taken unkindly by most of the members of the ABPC board, who had little or no interest in the international scene. Nevertheless, after much argument the board voted to renew the U.S. membership but to deny responsibility for the lapsed dues. (Indeed, it was proposed that the United States should have only a special "associate" membership and pay only half of the regular dues!) For several years thereafter, the board had an annual hassle over payment of the dues, which were never large in amount.

As more and more U.S. publishers became active in international markets, the opposition to the ABPC membership in the IPA diminished rapidly in the 1950s and early 1960s. Also the IPA itself changed, becoming more truly international and less dominated by its European members. A more subtle influence was the glamour of successive and ever-larger congresses in such old-world cities as Florence, Rome, Vienna, and Barcelona. The fame of these Continental gatherings as brilliant social occasions spread rapidly among the wives of American publishers, and this caused an industry-wide awakening to the apparent importance of the IPA. So much so that the American presence all but dominated the nineteenth congress at Paris in 1972. And over 60 representatives of 25 U.S. publishing houses attended the twentieth congress which gathered in Japan in 1976. How times and attitudes do change!

Considering the historical indifference of the book industry toward trade association activities, one has to ask why some publishers have been willing to give so freely of their time and energy in support of such activities. Is it because they are "joiners" by nature? Or that they have an uninhibited itch for leadership and peer recognition? Or that they instinctively desire to engage in group activities? Or do they believe, simply and genuinely, that they can improve the general quality and effectiveness of their chosen occupation? The answer, I suppose, lies usually in a combination of these and other motivations that may be peculiar to the individual. In any case, there have been, always, a few shakers and movers who have done most of the work of the book publishers associations. And it seems, too, that the spirit of leadership in industry matters becomes ingrained in certain houses whose officers are inclined to work almost as much for the general welfare as for the benefit of their own firms. This is a curious behavioral phenomenon, indeed, but lacking it the book industry certainly would have no trade association.

For myself, I think that most of us who have worked long and hard on our trade-association affairs must agree with John Donne's stern view of ontology—we believe that every firm in our industry is "a piece of the maine," and that anything that affects the industry for good or ill affects every firm in it accordingly. Or, to put it another way, we believe that no firm in the industry can be better than, or much above, the industry as a whole. It follows, then, that working to improve and strengthen book publishing is also working for individual benefits. And, what is more, I am sure that many of us feel an obligation—a debt of gratitude, maybe—to the industry that has given us so much career happiness and satisfaction.

So much for attitudes and motivations. Now what are the uses of a book publishers' trade association—of the AAP in the present case?

Following is a random listing of the major functions of the AAP as they have been expanded and strengthened, more or less, in recent years.

To carry on continuous programs that increase our knowledge of the industry and improve its practices in such operating areas as statistical reports, markets and marketing, exporting, copyright and permissions procedures, accounting and financial methods, credit and collection problems, employer/employee relations, and recruitment and training of personnel.

To promote the value of books to society and to encourage reading as a lifetime habit.

To serve as a sounding board and a mouthpiece for the industry in its relations with other industries and with the news and opinion media. The need to educate the latter *about* the book industry is great.

To deal jointly in matters of common interest with professional societies of authors, artists, educators, librarians, and scientists and other kinds of scholars. Here, again, there is a critical need to educate peripherally interested groups *about* publishing policies, practices, and economics.

To deal in trade-related matters with associations of booksellers, book manufacturers, and suppliers of paper and other book-production materials.

To communicate with the U.S. Congress and state legislatures concerning proposed new or revised legislation that would directly affect the book industry.

To work with government agencies at all levels in advising on their policies for regulating such matters as taxation, import duties, postal rates, competition with private enterprise, copyright registration, and the procurement of copyrights or copyrighted works for government use.

To advise and assist federal and state agencies in the planning and administration of their book-related programs.

To represent our industry and our national interests in dealings with the publishers' associations of other countries, with international agencies such as UNESCO, and with the international copyright organizations.

To organize the industry's assistance to book-development programs in the developing nations of the world.

To coordinate U.S. participation in the many book "fairs" that are organized each year in other countries and regions of the world.

To fight censorship of any kind and to oppose all attempts to abridge First Amendment rights to publish freely.

Given these major activities and many minor ones besides, the volunteer officers and the paid staff of the AAP have a very full plate year in and year out. Most of the important tasks are now well done, but a few continue to suffer neglect through either lack of funds or choice of short-term over long-term benefits. Further, priorities have had to change, of course, with changing times and shifting pressures. The greatest change of recent years has been the pronounced shift to more interest and activity in government relations. This has been concomitant with the rise of Big Government and of increased confrontation with it on several important fronts. This Washington-centered activity is now so extensive and crucial as to warrant separate treatment in the next chapter.

Another area that has grown rapidly in importance and coverage is international relations. Here, for a change, the industry's interests have been quite well looked after in recent years, and it now appears that the industry may be prepared to support the organization of an international center for the development of book publishing. This center would function on a pattern similar in many respects to that of the British Council in its support of British publishing in most areas of the world. As suggested in the preceding chapter, the need for such a center to operate outside the sphere of governmental influence has long been apparent both at home and abroad.

A third area that has demanded increased attention is our relationship with educators and librarians. As noted earlier, these relations have been strained—at times almost to the breaking point—by the long-drawn-out battle over revision of the copyright law. It seems likely that this unfortunate tension will have to be looked after carefully for several years to come.

Although the book industry can rejoice in the recent programmatic growth of the AAP and in the added support that its effective management has attracted, there are several important matters that still suffer neglect. The most important, in my view, is the need to mount an effective industry-wide program for product promotion—for selling the public on the high societal value of books. Usually, this kind of product advertising is a prime concern of a trade association, but as noted in an earlier chapter, the book industry has been historically indifferent to it. Broadly speaking, this is, of course, a public relations activity, and many publishers are at last becoming aware of its importance.

Another concern that cries out for industry-wide attention is the need to encourage, if not to support, technological advances for book production and distribution. Here the industry has been content to ride on the coattails of a few firms (publishers and printers) that have financed limited research-and-development programs.

A third concern that needs more constant and effectual attention is the "watchdog" function of guarding against unwarranted government competition with private-enterprise publishing. Here the need for constant vigilance and prompt action is ever present, yet the industry generally has never evidenced an awareness of the problem, much less organized a solid defense of its position. Rather, it has depended upon the alertness of a few specially interested publishers, who have rushed about, individually, in the role of flash-fire fighters. Thus the defense of the industry's interests has been sporadic and haphazard, responding only to crisis situations. Surely we need a much better-ordered effort in this important area.

A fourth concern is the need for the AAP to assume a leading and directing role in educating people in, for, and about book publishing. This need was clearly and forcibly stated in the report of the Education for Publishing Committee, which was cited and commended in the first two chapters of this book. It appears that the AAP is prepared to support the committee's recommendation that a center for education and training be established as soon as feasible. Again, this is a very heartening prospect.

Substantial help with certain other problems can be expected from the Book Industry Study Group, which was organized in 1976 with Andrew H. Neilly of John Wiley & Sons as chairman. The purpose of this organization is to try to find solutions to problems that transcend the several sectors of the book world—authors, publishers, manufacturers, materials suppliers, wholesalers, retail booksellers, college bookstores, and libraries and other institutional buyers of books. Memberships are drawn from all these sectors on a dues-paying basis. Four projects were undertaken in the first year. Three technical studies were completed: an analysis of the informational needs of the book industry; an examination and forecast of availability of paper for books over a two-year period; and a survey of library acquisition prospects through 1981. The fourth project was an open forum on the outlook on paper supply, based on the technical study.

In its second year, the group has mounted three other major projects, all scheduled for early completion. They are: a feasibility analysis of a book manufacturing capacity/loading study; a study of consumer book-buying habits and trends; and a survey of book industry trends, including general economic conditions, conditions in the various segments of the industry, and a description of various research studies bearing on the industry. The trends study is planned to be the first of an annual series of such appraisals.

Technical studies such as these should be very valuable to almost all book publishers for they will help us to identify and try to correct some serious operating weaknesses of our industry. Indeed, their need and value are well attested by the fact that in its first year and a half of existence, the Book Industry Study Group has grown to more than 40 members, including many leading commercial firms and several trade associations.

If the AAP and the Book Industry Study Group are to carry through all these heretofore neglected major tasks, plus a few additional ones of lesser importance, they will, to be sure, have to grow in size and resources. The industry can well afford to support such growth, but unfortunately many publishers still are penny-wise in their view of trade-association expense. In fact, a good number of AAP members think that their annual dues already are far too high. They are the ones, typically, who pay their dues and sit on the sidelines year after year. Not being on the field of play, they have but scant knowledge of the scope and importance of what their trade association does for the good of the book industry. They fail to relate, and in this failure they are to be more pitied than censured.

19

Taking Care
of the Government

Without knowing it, book publishers in the past decade have increasingly embraced the philosophy of Woodrow Wilson, who declared many years ago, "No government has ever been beneficent when the attitude of government was taking care of the people. The only freedom consists in people taking care of the government." This is to say that, after years of lethargy, the book industry at last became alert and aggressive in its confrontations with Big Government. The change was forced as the Federal government loomed larger and larger as a participant, competitor, regulator, and legislator in the business of book publishing. It culminated in the transfer of AAP headquarters from New York to Washington in 1973. That move signaled the industry's awakened determination to take care of the government, not to let the government take care of it.

Some of us old-timers in the industry had thought we might not live long enough to see that awakening. Our memories went back to the 1950s when the ABPC had to struggle to support a single professional staff member and his secretary in Washington. Theirs was largely a passive watchdog function, observing and reporting on all legislative and regulatory matters that were of interest and importance to the book industry. Active lobbying was proscribed because, as noted earlier, several influential members of the council considered it to be an unworthy or even dangerous kind of activity. But that Washington office did perform a service that was very useful to the book industry as a whole. For this reason, the ATPI board reluctantly agreed, in time, to share a small part of the expense. It was, to be sure, a hard, niggling agreement, and for a decade or more it was challenged every year at ATPI annual meetings. Many of the large schoolbook publishers disliked both the cost and the purpose of the arrangement. Strangely enough, they wanted no part of "meddling" in government affairs in Washington. They appeared to have no qualms whatever about going regularly in force to state capitals to pressure officials and committees for textbook adoptions or for appointments of friends to positions of influence, yet they abhorred the idea of lobbying, or of anything akin to it, at the Federal level. So every year they stoutly opposed the inclusion of $10,000 in the ATPI budget for sharing the expense of the ABPC Washington office. Beating down their opposition was the lively task of certain publishers who were members of both the ABPC and the ATPI. And it was not until 1966 that the Washington office was finally accepted as a joint responsibility and its cost ($40,000) shared equally by the two associations.

The foregoing account is given as perspective; it is only a part of the story of the book industry's slow acceptance of the importance of government relations. Another part has been told in the earlier chapter on our late awakening to the problems of copyright revision. Still another part is the never-ending struggle over the maintenance of preferred postal rates for the shipment of books. In the 1940s and 1950s, a handful of larger publishers supported an independent committee that engaged in overt lobbying for a special fourth-class postal rate for books and other kinds of educational materials. The basic purpose was to ensure that books enjoyed parity with newspapers and magazines in preferred postal rates as a public service for the populace in its quest for information and knowledge. Still, many publishers looked upon the committee with misgiving, arguing that the book industry should not ask our government for special favors of any sort.

The earlier attitude toward lobbying on postal rates has changed markedly in recent years with increased awareness of the problem and with a sharp escalation in postal rates of all classes. In the past decade, the AAP has attentively exerted due influence on Congress and the U.S. Postal Service in behalf of the book industry and its customers, and at present it works hand in hand with the NEA (National Education Association), the ABA, the ALA, and other concerned organizations. Here the customer relationship is important because booksellers, libraries, and educational institutions pay the carriage charges on almost all book shipments. But, naturally, the higher costs, even when they are passed on to consumers, have an adverse effect on book purchases. The magnitude of the current problem can be measured by the fact that in 1975 the total cost of postage on books shipped by special-rate fourth-class mail was approximately $150 million. Currently scheduled increases in postal rates would increase this cost to about $231 million by 1979 for the same volume of units shipped. Obviously, much of this increase would have to be absorbed in library and other institutional budgets for book acquisitions, and this would, of course, reduce the purchase of books by that much.

Further, even higher hikes in fourth-class postal rates may lie ahead. It seems likely that the U.S. Postal Service (as now conducted as a self-sustaining enterprise) will be caught in a vicious cycle of necessary rate increases to compensate for volume decreases brought on by the rate increases. Already, there has been a sharp decline in magazine postage because certain magazine publishers have found less expensive systems of distribution in large metropolitan areas. Book publishers and their customers will have to follow suit unless the concept of partially subsidized public-service function is restored to fourth-class mail for books. (Some publishers already have shifted to United Parcel Service for small bulk shipments.) In any event, the push-and-pull on the public-service policy question probably will continue for some years to come, and the book industry must alertly attend to its interest while decisions are being made by Congress and the Postal Service administrative boards.

Another area of governmental relations where the book industry has recently needed defensive representation in Washington is taxation. Since 1973, publishers have been threatened by an Internal Revenue Service ruling that, if not reversed, could in time seriously impair their ability to cumulate adequate operating capital. This ruling barred the time-honored accounting practice of expensing research-and-development costs as incurred—and in our industry all editorial and production expenses are, of course, research-and-development costs. (Here production expense is defined as the cost of overseeing the manufacture of a book by an outside printer.) Clearly, the ruling treats the book industry differently from other industries, all of which are allowed to write off research-and-development expenses as incurred. The tax revision bill of 1976 ruled out retroactive application of the IRS ruling, which is to say that this or any similar regulation can be applied only to taxable years beginning after the regulations are issued. Though publishers were thus relieved of the possibility of enormous past liabilities, it remains to negotiate with the IRS on new regulations that will avoid the same discrimination in the future. It appears, then, that the threat may hang over us for several years to come. Since many millions of questioned tax dollars are involved, the issue is highly critical to the industry. It is, decidedly, a good example of why publishers need expert advocacy in Washington.

Another instance of the book industry's need for a constant watchdog capability on the banks of the Potomac is the issue of government competition with private enterprise. As remarked earlier, the defense of this issue has never been well organized; rather, it has been the now-and-then concern of a few individual publishers of scientific, technical, and educational books. On a broad and continuing front the defense has always been against encroachments on the private sector's "territorial imperative" by the GPO (Government Printing Office), which has long been advertised as "the world's largest publisher." Thus each instance of defense usually becomes a David-and-Goliath struggle, and this tends to put off many commercial publishers who have genuine grievances. Still, over the years there have been many slingshot encounters in Washington, and while David has often failed to slay Goliath, the running battle has kept the GPO from competing more directly and more harmfully with commercial publishers.

There is still another threat to the welfare of commercial publishing that must be alertly watched on the Washington front. This is the itch of certain influential bureaucrats to see the Federal establishment of national information systems in all the major disciplines of science and technology. Here the basic idea is that a government agency, or a government-financed professional society, should be the repository of all information (knowledge) in a given discipline of science or in a new cross-discipline area of technology. The supporting argument is double-pronged: first, the Federal government finances most of the country's research-and-development activity; second, it is the only way in which the rapidly growing corpus of scientific and technical knowledge can be managed effectively. It follows, of course, that the Federally financed central repository would be, in each case, the purveyor of the information, in whatever form, to the public.

Not long ago, I heard a highly placed bureaucrat propose this particular scheme for centralized control to an approving audience of information scientists. As he saw it, the designated government agencies and professional societies would in time become the holders and "wholesalers" of all scientific and technical information, and the "retailers" of such information (the private publishers) would have to go to the wholesalers for what they needed. When questioned, the speaker admitted that he could not just then foresee the terms and conditions under which the sole-source wholesalers would dole out information to competitive retailers, but he was confident that all could be arranged fairly. He seemed to envision a kind of benevolent live-and-let-live coexistence of government control and commercial publishing. I applauded one aspect of his attitude, remarking that most bureaucrats would want the government to retail the monopolized information to all comers at nominal prices. At the same time, I realized that his proposed scheme had to be taken seriously. It was typical of many similar ones that are considered sympathetically in Washington each year by big-government advocates in the executive branch and in both houses of Congress as well. The book industry would do well to pay attention to them more constantly.

So far this discussion has placed government and book publishers in adversary roles—more so than is warranted, perhaps. There is, of course, another side to the relationship. This is the consultative/conciliatory side, where one can hopefully observe an increasing effort to work for mutual interests and the public good. For many years, the National Science Foundation has sought the advice of publishers—first by a committee on publishing policy, later by membership in the statutorily created Science Information Council. Likewise, the Atomic Energy Commission (now known as the Energy Research and Development Administration) appointed a standing committee of book and journal publishers to advise on its publishing policies and practices. Also, the U.S. Office of Education has, from time to time, asked publishers to serve on *ad hoc* committees appointed to consult on the administration of its book- and library-assistance programs.

Over the years, the U.S. Copyright Office has always consulted closely with book publishers, both individually and collectively, in its key role in guiding the revision of U.S. copyright law—a collaboration that has been very helpful to all concerned.

But of all the governmental departments and agencies that formally consult book publishers, the State Department has by far the best record. The Government Advisory Committee on International Book Programs was organized in 1962. Some ten years later, its purview was changed to include librarians and literary programs. The primary purpose of this committee was to advise on the relevant activities of the USIA and the AID, both wards of the State Department. It served many other uses in the department when called upon, and it also helped to inform many book publishers on the political mores and the operating policies and methods of Federal agencies. More than 50 publishing executives served terms on this committee, and certainly their service was of as much benefit to the book industry as to the government. Yet, alas, the Government Advisory Committee was scuttled in 1977 by the OMB (Executive Office of Management and Budget). This was done with the full approval of the then-current operating officers of AID and USIA, who apparently no longer wanted a "private-sector" advisory group looking over their shoulders. But I predict that, in good time, the State Department will find needs to reestablish this committee or to devise new but similar means for reviewing and guiding the book and library programs of its two ward agencies.

Another State Department advisory group has long been as helpful to our industry as to the government. This is the Advisory Panel on International Copyright, on which two book publishers serve by custom. Appointed by the Business Affairs Office, this panel often has been effective in helping the responsible government officials to look after the legal and commercial interests of U.S. copyright owners as affected by international treaties, protocols, and regulations. Fortunately, this advisory group survived the OMB cost/effectiveness review of 1977.

Still another instance of invited government consultation occurred in 1976 when the newly appointed Librarian of Congress named eight public-spirited book publishers as an *ad hoc* committee to advise his office on technical matters connected with a task-force study of that institution's wide and complex operations.

Perhaps the most significant signs of the book industry's political maturity were the recent organization of a Political Action Committee and the establishment of a program of open forums for continuing dialogue between government officials and publishers who have special interests in the Washington scene. The former is an independent group that lines up support for political candidates who are known to be sympathetic to cultural and educational affairs in the Federal government. The latter, an activity of the AAP, is designed to induce informal exchanges of ideas and views between the public and private sectors. Both activities were instigated by the president of the AAP, Townsend W. Hoopes, who has brought a high degree of political awareness and astuteness to his office.

If I were called upon to characterize the value of most of the book industry's advisory service to government agencies, I would reply, "They also serve who only watch and wait—and negate." This is to say that in most instances the value derives from the watchdog function—from constant watching for ideas and proposed programs that need to be barked at and chased away from the door. To put it bluntly, the greatest value of the advisory function is, more often than not, the achievement of negative results.

Naturally, many people in the book industry do not understand, or even know about, this negatory function. So they often complain that they see no programmatic action by the several advisory committees that work year after year with Federal agencies. They forget that the function of these committees is almost wholly consultative and advisory. And, of course, they never see, or hear about, most of the negations—about the frequent blocking of proposed ideas, policies, and programs that patently would be unneeded or impractical or even counterproductive. Neither do they realize that the negatory function is especially important in Washington where harebrained ideas and faulty plans can spring up like weeds—where there usually is a high rate of turnover of decision-making officials, and where the need for knowledgeable, memory-stored standing advisory committees is commensurately great.

Happily, book publishers are at last beginning to learn how to deal with Big Government—how to take care that the caretaking works both ways in Washington.

20

Is the Book Here to Stay?

A fashionable topic for discussion in the intellectual world today is "Is the book doomed?" Or, stated more fatally, "Is the book dying?" Put either way, the question is a surefire activator for a lively cocktail or dinner conversation, or for a speech or article, or even for a symposium, seminar, or colloquim. Almost everywhere I go, at home or abroad, I am asked—twittingly by the young, anxiously by the no-longer-young—whether it is true that the years of the book are numbered. In some instances, the question is put more elegantly: "Is it true that the new communications technology is rapidly making the book an obsolescent form of information transfer?" In others, less elegantly: "Won't you Gutenberg-era boys soon fold under the impact of the computer and the new electron-optical gadgets?"

No matter how such questions are put, or how much they may vary in their innocence or sophistication, they add up to an aroused intellectual interest in the fate of the book. The extent of this interest was indicated a few years ago by a very sober international symposium entitled "Doom of the Book?" that attracted some 300 intellectuals to Zürich as guests of the Duttweiler Institute, a foundation dedicated to the study of political and social problems. This is but one of the many, many manifestations of the lively concern that one now encounters everywhere among book-minded people.

I suppose that most publishers have by now developed, as I have, a stock response to questions on the subject. Mine starts with the thesis that there is no such thing as "the book," either alive, or doomed, or dying. Rather, there are in fact many kinds of books, and the vulnerability of each kind must be considered separately. When thus considered, certain kinds—and only a few—appear to be vitally threatened by the new technology; other kinds are not, and probably will not be so threatened in the foreseeable future. Which, then, are the threatened kinds?

First would come the kind that comprises exact and discrete bits of information that can easily be put into a computerated system for retrieval by users who know exactly what they want. These are books of numerical tables and formulas and of other technical and statistical data that are so widely used in science, engineering, business, and industry. It seems to be only a matter of time until all such data and information will be supplied in all industrially advanced countries by computer-based electron-optical systems and not by book publishers. (And how will users in undeveloped countries then be served?)

Second in line comes the kind of books that are widely used as reference tools—volumes of indexes, bibliographies, citations, thesauri, directories, and the like, all of which also lend themselves readily to mechanized storage-and-retrieval systems. Here the fate of the printed volume probably will be determined in each case by two factors—frequency of use and the ability of users to pay the cost of conversion to mechanical systems.

Third in line are reference books containing entries that are short, concise, and factual—works such as specialized dictionaries, glossaries, encyclopedias, abstracts, and concordances, in which the user's exact need can be easily identified and quickly supplied by computer printout or electron-optical display. Again the frequency of use and the cost of conversion are the factors that will control the rate at which printed volume publication is outmoded.

Still another species of book has recently become endangered by the application of a different kind of technology. This is the specialized treatise or monograph that is today so widely and liberally photocopied in part for private study or for interlibrary "loan" in lieu of the book itself. Most publishers are convinced that these reprographic practices—and especially those that are systematically organized—are responsible for a precipitous decline in the sales of such books, which if not somehow checked, will surely make their publication economically impossible within a few years.

The foregoing prediction is prompted by the occurrence of what I have called by analogy the "twigging phenomenon" in the publication of scientific monographs. A good number of years ago I described this phenomenon as the continual fractionation of scientific knowledge and, hence, of the subject matter of scientific books. Naturally, this endless fractionation results in scores of highly specialized books being written each year for groups of readers that are no larger today than they were 25 years ago, despite the fact that our total population of scientists has more than quadrupled in the past quarter century.

In my analogy, the subjects of such books represent twigs on the tree of scientific knowledge. Although the tree itself is perhaps 5 times larger than it was 25 years ago, the twigs are still the same size—and so are the markets for specialized books. The trunk of the tree, representing basic textbooks and handbooks, is much larger, of course. So are the main limbs and secondary boughs, representing intermediate textbooks and general treatises. Both kinds of scientific books are sold in much larger numbers. But for the "twig" books—the advanced treatises and monographs—the market has not increased at all.

The rub comes, of course, when the current, much higher initial plant costs have to be spread over the same number of copies as that printed many years ago. This kind of squeeze does not occur in the production of a textbook, for example, where even a 100 percent increase in plant costs can be leveled out by a print order two or three times as big as it would have been 25 years ago. But the twig books have to bear the economic curse of continual fractionation of markets. And their prices will continue to be disproportionately high if scientists are to be served adequately in their professional literature.[1]

As noted earlier, there is convincing evidence that in many library systems one copy of such a book now suffices where five or ten copies were needed a few years ago. And there is the prospect that, with the rapid growth of state and regional library networks—all interlinked by computer-based operational systems—one very high-priced copy will soon serve in place of 50 or 100 copies. Thus it seems inevitable that monographs and specialized treatises will be forced to extinction unless photocopying can be brought under control by legal or voluntary means. Here the fate of the printed work will be determined by whether or not copyright protection can be effectively applied.

Thus, in my view, only the publishers of specialized technical and scholarly works and of small-bit reference works have present cause to worry about the future viability of their products. No other kind of book seems to be in real danger of obsolescence at the hand of the nonprint communications technology that is known today. This is because the book remains the most efficient and economical system for the storage and retrieval of almost all kinds of "non-bit" information that are in extensive use. Also, as a literary package, the book is the best medium for presenting lengthy works intended for instruction, entertainment, enlightenment, or inspiration—works that need to be read thoughtfully, contemplatively, reflectively, even ruminatively. Mechanized information systems and audiovisual entertainment products have failed to match these advantages and virtues of the book.

Another signal advantage of the book is that it is so eminently portable. It can easily be taken almost anywhere at any time. It can be quickly taken up and quickly put away again. It will travel in a pocket or under the arm or in school satchels, briefcases, flight bags, knapsacks, shopping baskets, glove compartments, and even in the oversize handbags and cases that both men and women carry nowadays. Abe Lincoln often stowed a book in his stovepipe hat, and before him an eccentric nineteenth century scholar habitually carried a book in his cap wherever he went. And, of all things, Lord Chesterfield a century earlier solemnly counseled his son always to take a book with him when "The calls of nature oblige a pass to the necessary-house." Characteristically, Chesterfield followed this bit of counsel with more precise advice: "Books of science and of a grave sort must be read with continuity; but there are very many, and even very useful ones, which may be read with advantage by snatches and unconnectedly: such are all the good Latin poets, except Virgil in his *Aeneid*, and such are most of the modern poets, in which you will find many pieces worth reading that will not take up above seven or eight minutes." Then this preceptor of elegant behavior went on to describe the habit of a friend who had gone through all the Latin poets in this way: "He bought, for example, a common edition of Horace, of which he tore off gradually a couple of pages, carried them with him to that necessary-place, read them first, and then sent them down as a sacrifice to Cloacina." With such eminent historical testimony to the fact, one has to conclude that convenience and portability combined have always given the book its strongest survival characteristic.

The book has still another decisive advantage over the mechanized media—it allows the reader, or the prospective reader, to browse freely in its content or among a collection of similar works. This is a felicity that is highly cherished by many general readers and by all scholars and researchers. Indeed, it is the main reason why most scholars and researchers prefer to work in libraries rather than with mechanized information systems.

Finally, when the book is fixed in place as a component of a learning or information system (or, in plain words, placed on the shelf), its maintenance cost is negligible. It asks only to be dusted off now and then and to be protected as needed against cockroaches and other starch-hungry predators that might want to feast on its binding. But, of course, this is not an important matter because with most book buyers the problem is not to preserve what they have; rather, it is to choose what they must get rid of. This familiar problem in itself says a great deal about the abiding attraction of books.

Often when a publisher is quizzed on the future of his industry, the leadoff question is about the impact of television on the reading of books. Although the reply can be based on presumptive evidence only, most publishers do not hesitate to assert that television has rather increased then decreased the buying and reading of books, even among youngsters who spend untold hours in front of the TV screen. This deviation from expected behavior is explained by the assumption that television viewing frequently stimulates intellectual interests or awakens literary tastes that can be satisfied only by turning to books. This is, to be sure, only a rationalized explanation of the fact that book sales were not in the least diminished with the advent of heavy TV viewing. However, we do have recent concrete evidence that certain popular TV series can stimulate high sales of accompanying books. For example, Kenneth Clark's *Civilization,* Alistair Cooke's *America*, Bronowski's *Ascent of Man*, *The Adams Family Chronicle*, and Haley's *Roots* caused viewers to buy copies of the related books by the hundreds of thousands. What is more, popular motion pictures based on books often have boomed sales of "movie" paperback reprints of the original works by the millions of copies.

Now, as to possible adjustments of the book industry to the new technologies of reprography and electronic transmission of information, a number of publishers have given much thought and some investigation of certain indicated new modes of publishing. The possibility of publishing highly specialized works in micrographic form—by microfilm, microfiche, or microprint—has been investigated hopefully with the thought that original publication in such form might be practicable for producing editions that are too small to fit the economy of traditional book production. To date this form has been successfully employed only for republication of out-of-print works—for serials and other large volumes of collected papers and for multivolume classics that were first published in book form. Here the profitable ventures have been massive and high-priced packages that are sold by subscription in advance of publication.

In the past decade, a few commercial firms and two or three university presses have experimented with microform publishing of current single-volume works, and the result in nearly every case has been economic failure. This failure can be attributed to several factors: first, user resistance, which is caused largely by the fact that effective and moderately priced reader/printers have not yet been perfected; second, marketing and fulfillment costs, which are unbearably high in relation to acceptable levels of sales price; and third, the slowness of "on-demand" sales, which are neither immediate enough nor large enough in dollar volume to invite entrepreneurial investment. In short, the technology of the software is acceptable, but that of the hardware is not, while both the economics of pricing and the high cost of sales and sales service to the individual customer are impossible. But in spite of current failures, some book publishers still believe that micrographics will one day be widely used for several kinds of limited-edition works. Certainly, continued experimentation with the medium can be expected. Come what may, those information specialists and all others who have urged microform publishing upon the book industry should understand that here operational costs constitute a critical barrier to the attainment of what has long been technologically feasible.

Along the same time, a few publishers have less hopefully looked into the feasibility of on-demand publishing in traditional hard-copy format. This assumes a system whereby copies of books, or parts thereof, would be printed only after they have been ordered. The publisher produces a master copy, either full-size or in microform, and photoduplicates are made to fill orders on demand, one at a time. Thus, it is argued, the costs of warehousing, carrying inventory, and unsold inventory write-offs are avoided. Also, the initial investment is small, so there is little risk, and the loss is minimal if the work does not sell well. Accordingly, more works of limited interest can be published with the same amount of investment capital and less loss of funds.

Unfortunately, those who are promoting the idea of on-demand publishing (mostly librarians and the so-called information scientists) have ignored some very serious economic obstacles. The largest of these are the high cost of obtaining and servicing small-quantity orders, and the even higher cost of processing production to fill each of such orders. (For scholarly books about 40 percent of the total cost of edition publishing is production cost; for on-demand publishing the proportion would decrease to only 20 or 30 percent. In short, the concept of on-demand publishing implies a reversion to cottage-industry economy.

One knowledgeable investigator of the economics of on-demand publishing, Herbert S. Bailey, Jr., director of Princeton University Press, has made the following observation: "It will be seen that . . . the total costs of on-demand publishing and of edition publishing are the same at about 166 copies. If the expected demand is above this level, edition publishing will be more efficient; below this level on-demand publishing should be preferred. . . . My purpose . . . is to point out the *limits* of on-demand publishing, the false assumptions of many on-demand enthusiasts, and the damage to scholarly communication that may result if on-demand techniques are adopted where they are not suitable."[2]

Finally, looking farther ahead, one must ask how will the book fare when we come to the ultimate of modern information systems—the totally mechanized library of the future, the library in which all knowledge will be stored in electronic memory banks and retrieved on demand in instant hard-copy printout form or by lightning-speed electron-optical screen display.

I suggest that the time has not yet come for publishers and authors to worry seriously about this prospective kind of displacement of printed books. Here my persuasion is based rather on considerations of human nature and economics than on prospects of technological potentials. Surely, ordinary readers—and students and scholars and teachers as well—will continue to insist on the convenience, flexibility, and other amenities that the book affords. Obviously, any mechanized library that depends on microform storage must have printed pages to copy in the first place; thus it will have to depend on books for most of its input. (It is hard to imagine that creative writers, other than certain scientists and engineers, would produce works solely for storage in mechanized libraries.) And, presumably, any mechanized library that stores the total content of all its books and other publications in computer-controlled memory banks will be exceedingly costly to establish and operate. It is this economic factor—a combination of prohibitive start-up costs and high operational expense—that is likely, more than any other, to save the book from the technological obsolescence that some librarians and information scientists and equipment manufacturers are predicting.

Nevertheless, neither the place of books in American society nor the future welfare of the industry that produces them can be taken for granted. Publishers must face the fact that promoters of the new technological modes of communication will try, subtly or otherwise, to discount or write off books as being dinosaurian in both form and function. And it must be recognized that the new modes do have an undeniable glamour that gives them certain advantages whenever economic or political considerations are involved, e.g., the right of ready access to copyrighted materials. Also, the recent emphasis on the public's "right to know," coupled with the strong demand for "free flow of information," can damage the proprietary interests of the book industry. (Far too many people seem to think that "free flow of information" means "flow of free information.") It seems, then, that publishers should extend themselves to fortify the competitive position of the book as an indispensable instrument of information, education, culture, and inspiration. One can hope that the oncoming new generation of publishers will have a more competitive spirit and will make a substantial effort to promote the societal value of their products. For without an abundance of books—more and more of every kind for more and more readers everywhere—the world would surely become a stale and dreary place indeed.

Notes and References

CHAPTER 1

1. For an interesting account of book publishing and bookselling in colonial America, see John Tebbel, *A History of Book Publishing in the United States*, Vol. 1 (New York: Bowker, 1972), pp. 13–47.

2. Fredric Warburg, *An Occupation for Gentlemen*, 2nd ed. (London: Hutchinson & Co., 1959).

3. Association of American Publishers, Education for Publishing Committee, *The Accidental Profession: Education, Training and the People of Publishing* (New York: Association of American Publishers, 1977), p. 11.

4. Ibid.

5. Ibid., p. 45.

CHAPTER 2

1. Association of American Publishers, Education for Publishing Committee, *The Accidental Profession: Education, Training and the People of Publishing* (New York: Association of American Publishers, 1977), p. 13.

2. Ibid., p. 23.

3. Ibid., p. 17.

4. Ibid., p. 15.

5. Ibid., p. 78. This quotation is from a highly informative section, "Publishing and Education Abroad," contributed by Desmond F. Reaney of the R. R. Bowker Company. His description of the system for truly professional training of both publishers and booksellers in West Germany could serve as an approach to better education for publishing in the United States. *Fachschule des Deutschen Buchhandels* emphasizes the commercial side of the country's booktrade as a whole, rather than any of its separate parts, such as publishing, bookselling, or librarianship.

6. The U.S. Department of Commerce estimates that fifty to sixty thousand people are currently employed in book publishing. The number peaked in 1973 and has declined slightly since then. Only about 16 percent of the total are employed in what the Bureau of Labor Statistics classified as "professional" jobs.

CHAPTER 3

1. One astute publisher, Samuel Vaughn of Doubleday, has suggested that the advent of the Xerox copying machine has abetted this rebellion. Now several copies of a manuscript can be made quickly and cheaply for simultaneous submission to several publishers.

2. Several cases of author-publisher friendships are very interestingly and sensitively described in Charles A. Madison, *Irving to Irving: Author-Publisher Relations, 1800–1974* (New York: Bowker, 1974).

CHAPTER 4

1. See especially Charles A. Madison, *Book Publishing in America* (New York: McGraw-Hill, 1966). Use the index references as a guide to people and companies herein mentioned.

2. Quoted from Alfred A. Knopf, *Publishing Then and Now*, Bowker Memorial Lectures No. 21 (New York: New York Public Library, 1964), p. 9.

3. Madison, *Book Publishing in America*.

4. Speaking of the usual author's ego and sensitivity, Samuel Vaughn of Doubleday recently remarked upon one of the many things taught by his chief editor and friend, Ken McCormick. "Never write on an author's original manuscript until you know him well," he cautioned. "It can be like writing on his skin." See Samuel Vaughn, *Medium Rare: A Look at the Book and Its People*, Bowker Memorial Lectures New Series No. 4 (New York: Bowker, 1976), p. 14.

CHAPTER 5

1. For a fair and judicious account of this much-publicized affair, see the final chapter of Charles A. Madison, *Irving to Irving: Author-Publisher Relations, 1800–1974* (New York: Bowker, 1974).

CHAPTER 6

1. These estimates were supplied by industry economists and verified, where possible, by trade association sources. Exact figures are hard to come by.

2. These records of profitability were extracted from recent annual *Industry Statistics* reports to the AAP, prepared by John P. Dessauer, Inc. Before 1975 the details of these reports were held confidential, but the top figures were released for publication. Since 1975, copies of the report have been freely sold by the AAP. They are a mine of information about the U.S. book industry.

3. An estimate by Edward E. Booher of McGraw-Hill in a lecture entitled "What Has Happened to the Intellectual Entrepreneurs?" given at the Columbia University School of Business on February 19, 1974.

4. R. R. Bowker's annual *Literary Market Place* is an indispensable directory of information on American book publishing and related agencies, associations, trades, suppliers, etc. Bowker produces a companion annual directory, *International Literary Market Place*, which is equally valuable to publishers who are involved in overseas operations.

CHAPTER 7

1. "Editorial," *Publishers Weekly*, September 16, 1950, p. 1125.

2. Quoted from an interview with Roger W. Straus, Jr., *Publishers Weekly*, February 7, 1977, p. 55. A leading publisher of literary titles,

Mr. Straus was speaking mainly of general books, of course. The publishers of other kinds—textbooks and professional books, in particular—had put up their prices to realistic levels some years earlier.

CHAPTER 8

1. In 1977, the B. Dalton and Waldenbooks chains were reported to have 270 stores and 444 stores respectively. For the nonbook chain stores, the following numbers of book departments were reported: Wards, 460; Sears, 720; J. C. Penney, 2,055.

CHAPTER 9

1. The Children's Book Council office is located at 67 Irving Place, New York, N.Y. 10003. Inquiries about its programs and promotional material are invited.

2. "Educational Publishers Plan Campaign to Boost National Spending on Materials," *Publishers Weekly*, February 28, 1977, p. 66.

CHAPTER 10

1. John P. Dessauer, "Too Many Books," *Publishers Weekly*, September 20, 1974; "The Cult of Novelty and Its Fatal Consequences," *Publishers Weekly*, October 7, 1974; "Hazards of Overprinting and Inventory Inflation," *Publishers Weekly*, October 14, 1974. All were reprinted in an anthology, *The Business of Publishing* (New York: Bowker, 1976). Reprinted in the same volume were letters to *Publishers Weekly* (December 2, 1974) from three publishers who expressed strong contrary views, and an article by Anthony Netboy, "Too Many Books? An Author's Experience," *Publishers Weekly* (February 10, 1975), in which the author agreed with Mr. Dessauer's thesis. For the critical analysis, see Fritz Machlup, "They Don't Know They Are Sick," *Publishers Weekly*, September 29, 1975.

2. Quoted from Ben W. Huebsch, *Busman's Holiday*, R. R. Bowker Memorial Lectures No. 19 (New York: New York Public Library, 1959), p. 34.

3. Quoted from Alfred A. Knopf, *Publishing Then and Now*, R. R. Bowker Memorial Lectures No. 21 (New York: New York Public Library, 1964), p. 17.

4. See the *Bowker Annual of Library and Book Trade Information* (New York: Bowker, 1971), pp. 65 ff. The production figures now reported each year by the *Bowker Annual* and *Publishers Weekly* are based on Bowker's *Weekly Record*, which is far more comprehensive than were the *Publishers Weekly* listings of earlier years. Probably a correctional factor of 10–20 percent is needed to make the figures of the 1970s comparable with those of 20 or 30 years ago.

5. These numbers are unofficial estimates supplied by the U.S. Office of Education. The U.S. Bureau of the Census reports the following numbers of living college graduates 25 years old and over:

1960   7,625 million
1970   11,717 million
1975   16,244 million (est.)

Naturally, the numbers of graduates under the age of 25 are currently much larger than in earlier years. At present, the college-graduate population has a net increase of about 1,000,000 per year.

6. Association of American Publishers, Education for Publishing Committee, *The Accidental Profession: Education, Training and the People of Publishing* (New York: Association of American Publishers, 1977), p. 30.

CHAPTER 11

1. The production figures shown in this tabulation were derived from Bowker's *Weekly Record* and published in the Annual Summary Numbers of *Publishers Weekly*. A comment on their historical comparability can be found in Chapter 10, Note 4.

2. C. P. Snow, *The Two Cultures and the Scientific Revolution* (New York: Cambridge University Press, 1959).

CHAPTER 12

1. Fritz Machlup, *The Production and Distribution of Knowledge in the United States* (Princeton, N.J.: Princeton University Press, 1962).

2. *Bowker Annual of Library and Book Trade Information* (New York: Bowker, 1977), p. 330.

CHAPTER 13

1. Quoted from an interview with William Jovanovich, *Publishers Weekly*, October 13, 1975, p. 22.

CHAPTER 14

1. The Copyright Act of 1976, officially entitled Public Law 94-553 (October 19, 1976) has been reprinted many times. Convenient sources for it are Don Johnston's *A Guide to the New Copyright Law* (New York: Bowker, 1978); the 22nd edition of the *Bowker Annual* (New York: Bowker, 1977), pp. 625 ff.; and the New York Law School *Law Review* (November 2, 1977), pp. 811 ff. The sets of guidelines for exempted library and classroom uses can be found in a booklet, *New Copyright Law: Overview*, written by Charles H. Lieb, Esquire and distributed by the Association of American Publishers, One Park Avenue, New York, N.Y. 10016. An enlarged and corrected edition was issued in July 1977.

2. In spite of the provisions of the new law and of the fact that several library associations formally accepted the accompanying set of guidelines, librarians generally are not reconciled to the requirements. A survey of 138 libraries made in 1977 by Knowledge Industry Publications, Inc., found the following: Only 1.4 percent of the librarians interviewed approved payment for each item copied; 4.3 percent would pay a surcharge for a book that would allow unlimited copying; 47.8 percent thought they should be able to copy excerpts without payment; 29.9 percent felt they should be allowed to make a single copy of anything without payment; 8.1 percent thought they should be able to copy with no restrictions whatever. Not surprisingly, the survey found that very few libraries keep careful records of copying done by either their staff or their patrons.

CHAPTER 17

1. Datus C. Smith, Jr., *The Economics of Book Publishing in Developing Countries*, Reports and Papers on Mass Communications No. 79 (Paris: UNESCO, 1977). Available from Unipub, New York, $2.

2. For many years, Franklin ran a clearing house for information on available rights for translation of U.S. books into the "noncommercial" languages of developing countries—a service that was taken over in 1974 by the AAP. At the start of 1978, the R. R. Bowker Company will begin IRIS (International Rights Information Service), which will disseminate globally information about available secondary rights of all kinds of U.S. books. If this service proves to be commercially feasible, it will be of great value to developing-country publishers and to many U.S. publishers as well, and especially to smaller firms that do not have staffs specializing in the sale of such rights.

3. Quoted from recent annual statements of the Franklin Corporation. Actually, Franklin has from time to time performed certain intermediary services that go beyond this set of general objectives. For example, Franklin field-office personnel have occasionally become directly involved in the management of local printing, binding, publishing, and distribution—wisely in some cases, unwisely in others.

CHAPTER 20

1. I first described this "phenomenon" in an article in the April 1952 issue of *Physics Today*. It attracted very little notice, however, until I redescribed it in an article entitled "Soaring Prices and Sinking Sales of Science Monographs" in the January 24, 1974 issue of *Science*. By then the squeeze between higher costs and lower sales was getting acute, so both scientists and librarians sat up and took notice of what was happening.

2. Herbert S. Bailey, Jr., "The Limits of On-Demand Publishing," *Scholarly Publishing* (July 1975), pp. 296, 298.

Bibliography

This compilation is not intended to be inclusive by any means. Rather, it is a listing of books and periodicals about book publishing, which the author has found to be particularly entertaining, instructive, or useful at one time or another.

BOOKS

General

Altbach, Philip G., and McVey, Sheila S., eds. *Perspectives on Publishing.* Philadelphia: American Academy of Political and Social Science, 1975; Lexington, Mass.: Lexington Books, 1976.

The entire contents of the September 1975 issue of *The Annals of the American Academy of Political and Social Science*, which was given over to topical and functional articles on book publishing, bookselling, and the place of books in American society and abroad. The articles are lively, timely, and provocative. Recommended for its humanistic flavor.

Bailey, Herbert S., Jr. *The Art and Science of Book Publishing.* New York: Harper & Row, 1970.

A knowledgeable and sophisticated treatise which applies management science to all aspects of its subject. Highly recommended for readers who are experienced in the business and are able to handle the author's mathematical formulations and analyses.

The Business of Publishing: A PW Anthology. Introduction by Arnold Ehrlich. New York: R. R. Bowker, 1976.

A collection of some of the most important articles on this aspect of publishing that appeared in *PW* between the years 1971 and 1976. A miscellany of current, topical discussions that make informative reading for anyone who is not a constant reader of *PW*.

Dessauer, John P. *Book Publishing: What It Is and What It Does.* New York: R. R. Bowker, 1974.

A concise guide to the practical operations of a book-publishing enterprise, written by a technician. Unfortunately, the author attempts to explain what happens in publishing in terms of statistical or operational analyses with too little attention to the human side.

Grannis, Chandler B., ed. *What Happens in Book Publishing*, 2nd ed. New York: Columbia University Press, 1967.

A book of 20 chapters, each written by an expert in a major function or category of publishing. The chapters are uneven in style and explication, but they add up to the best available orientation to the broad spectrum of the book industry.

Greenfield, Howard. *Books from Writer to Reader.* New York: Published by the author and distributed by Crown, 1976.

A concisely written and well-illustrated book that answers many practical questions about writing and publishing books. The author has broad experience in writing, editing, publishing, and selling books. A very useful primer.

Jovanovich, William. *Now, Barabbas.* New York: Harper & Row, 1964.

A philosophical book about the publisher's craft and his relationships with writers, readers, bankers, fellow publishers, and the public at large. The author is one of the country's most perceptive and articulate publishers, and this book is an intellectual delight.

Kujoth, Jean Spencer, comp. *Book Publishing: Inside Views.* Metuchen, N.J.: Scarecrow, 1971.

A miscellany of articles on the book industry that were published between 1962 and 1970. Interesting reading, but a few of the articles are both topically and factually out of date. Still most of them have either durable or historical value.

Smith, Datus C., Jr. *A Guide to Book Publishing*. New York: R. R. Bowker, 1966.

Though written for the instruction of publishers in developing countries, this unusually comprehensive manual is a valuable guide for newcomers to the book industry anywhere. The author was director of the Princeton University Press before he served for many years as president and chairman of Franklin Book Programs, whose staff contributed several specialized chapters to the book.

Smith, Roger H., ed. *The American Reading Public: What It Reads—Why It Reads*. New York: R. R. Bowker, 1964.

An expansion of the Winter 1963 issue of *Daedalus*, the journal of the American Academy of Arts and Sciences, which was devoted to books and book publishing in America. Some of the authoritative articles are now topically obsolete, but the whole issue still makes lively reading.

Unwin, Sir Stanley. *The Truth about Publishing*, 7th ed. New York: R. R. Bowker, 1960.

The classic work in its field, it was first published in 1926. The author dominated British publishing for four decades and in addition had an international reputation as the authority who first "removed mystery from publishing." The latter fact is attested to by the ten foreign-language translations of this book. Recommended for its historical interest and its strong expressions of British biases of the day.

Warburg, Frederic. *An Occupation for Gentlemen*. London: Hutchinson, 1959.

A mixture of publishing philosophy and methods and the author's experiences as a publisher, with emphasis on his relationships with his favored successful authors. It can be recommended for its revelation of the hauteur of so many of London's literary publishers and their commonly shared disdain for American publishing.

Author-Editor/Publisher Relations

Kuehl, John, and Bryer, Jackson, eds. *Dear Scott/Dear Max: The Fitzgerald-Perkins Correspondence*. New York: Scribner, 1971.

This highly interesting book is, in reality if not in form, a narrative of the relationship between a brilliant author and his guiding and steadying editor. It takes Fitzgerald from age 21, when he was writing his first book, *This Side of Paradise*, to his tragic death at age 43, when he was writing *The Last Tycoon*.

Madison, Charles A. *Irving to Irving: Author-Publisher Relations, 1800–1974*. New York: R. R. Bowker, 1974.

Instructive and often entertaining accounts of the friendships and hardships between notable authors and their publishers, ranging from Washington Irving's involvements with Mathew Carey in the first decade of the nineteenth century to Clifford Irving's "caper" with McGraw-Hill on the bogus biography of Howard Hughes in 1973 and 1974.

Biography

Canfield, Cass. *Up & Down & Around: A Publisher Recollects the Time of His Life*. New York: Harper & Row, 1971.

A distinguished publisher, who was for many years the head of the House of Harper, here reveals his relationships with the many distinguished authors whose works he published with relish and success.

Cerf, Bennett. *At Random: The Reminiscences of Bennett Cerf*. New York: Random House, 1977.

A posthumous memoir of a publisher who turned publicist and won fame as a raconteur, a compiler of joke books, and a TV "personality." This account was composed by the author's widow in collaboration with a former chief editor at Random, working largely from tapes in Columbia University's oral history collection. Presented in a highly personal and informal style, it offers entertainment but little else.

Doran, George. *Chronicles of Barabbas, 1884–1934*, 2nd ed. New York: Holt, Rinehart & Winston, 1952.

A classic work by one of the founders of the present-day Doubleday & Co. that has retained its entertaining and instructive values through many years.

Exman, Eugene. *The Brothers Harper*. New York: Harper & Row, 1965.

This informative and perceptive book is best described by its rather long subtitle: *A Unique Publishing Partnership and Its Impact upon the Cultural Life of America from 1817 to 1853*. It is hard to overstate the early influence of "that remarkable brotherhood," the four founding Harpers, but the author does his best.

Gilmer, Walker. *Horace Liveright: Publisher of the Twenties*. New York: David Lewis, 1970.

An entertaining biography of the most adventurous and flamboyant of American publishers of the twentieth century. The author's life and career in the book industry are properly treated in a legendary manner.

Haydn, Hiram. *Words & Faces*. New York: Harcourt Brace Jovanovich, 1974.

A sensitive and enlightening book about this scholarly author's life in publishing with emphasis on his authors and business associates. Especially interesting is the account of the founding of Atheneum Publishers and of the author's "disassociation" from his partnership in that firm.

Madison, Charles A. *The Owl among Colophons: Henry Holt as Publisher and Editor*. New York: Holt, Rinehart & Winston, 1966.

A biography published in honor of the firm's 100th anniversary. An interesting account of the founder's colorful life and of the early years of his company. The author was an editor in Holt's college department for almost 40 years. He emphasizes Holt's personal style of publishing and management.

Targ, William. *Indecent Pleasures*. New York: Macmillan, 1975.

Targ, a successful editor/publisher, writes an intimate account of persons and events in his career. It is informal and very readable, with frequent lacings of cynical or crusty remarks that give flavor to the author's sensible attitude toward writers, publishers, and the book trade in general.

Warburg, Frederic. *All Authors Are Equal*. New York: St. Martin's, 1973.

A memoir of an English publisher that is interesting but overly full of people and events in his personal life. It has value to the American reader as a revelation of the traditional style of publishing in London, and it clearly shows that some publishers can have egos that match those of their authors.

Williams, W. E. *Allen Lane: A Personal Portrait*. London: The Bodley Head, 1973.

A short and remarkably candid ("warts and all") biography of the founder of Penguin Books, who pioneered for the modern era the publishing of paperbacks throughout the English-speaking world. Highly recommended.

Company History

Burlingame, Roger. *Of Making Many Books.* New York: Scribner, 1946.

A very readable and perceptive account of the founding and early years of the aristocratic house, Charles Scribner's Sons. One of the very best books of its genre.

————. *Endless Frontiers: The Story of McGraw-Hill.* New York: McGraw-Hill, 1959.

Published in celebration of the McGraw-Hill Book Company's 50th anniversary, this history gives a very good account of the company's founders and its early years, but its later chapters are inadequate. Unfortunately, the author's health failed when the book was about half finished, and the quality of his work suffered accordingly.

Exman, Eugene. *The House of Harper: One Hundred and Fifty Years of Publishing.* New York: Harper & Row, 1967.

A thorough, but occasionally pedantic and overly laudatory, account of what the author calls "a biography" of the great House of Harper. Nevertheless a very informative book. The author's enthusiasm can be excused; he was for 35 years the editor-manager of Harper's religious book department.

Howard, Michael S. *Jonathan Cape, Publisher.* London: Jonathan Cape, 1971.

This is a mixture of biography of Cape and history of the firm which he founded with G. Wren Howard in 1921. Written in a lively style, but careful attention is given to important details. Entertaining reading from which an edifying picture of the British way of personal publishing emerges. The author's tone is a model of restraint.

Lawler, Thomas B. *Seventy Years of Textbook Publishing: A History of Ginn and Company.* Boston: Ginn, 1938.

This title has historical interest because it tells what textbook publishing was like in the early days. The author, one of many Ginn partners, writes in a style and posture that tells much about the schoolbook industry's image of itself in the first half of the century.

Matheson, Martin. *The First One Hundred and Fifty Years: A History of John Wiley and Sons, Inc.* New York: Wiley, 1957.

An unusual history in that it is told in terms of the company's most important books and in chapters contributed by its then-current authors and advisers. The plan is novel, but it fails to come off well. Several of the 28 contributions are dull and pedantic.

Nowell-Smith, Simon. *The House of Cassell*. London: Cassell, 1958.

A well-written, straight-on history of one of England's largest and most diversified houses, which was founded in 1848. It tells the story of the management's philosophy of expansion and acquisition, which predated by two or three decades the American urge in the same direction. Thus this history is the antithesis of that of Jonathan Cape, Ltd.

Copyright

Johnston, Don. *A Guide to the New Copyright Law*. New York: R. R. Bowker, 1978.

A comprehensive, nontechnical work that has great value to anyone in publishing who has to deal with copyright matters under the provisions of the Copyright Act of 1976. The author is counsel to the R. R. Bowker Company and is on the legal staff of the Xerox Publishing Division.

Kent, Allen, and Lancour, Harold, eds. *Copyright: Current Viewpoints on History, Laws, Legislation*. New York: R. R. Bowker, 1972.

A series of articles drawn from the *Encyclopedia of Library and Information Science*. Though somewhat outdated by the enactment of the Copyright Act of 1976, this volume retains considerable value for its discussions of various views on current problems of copyright protection, not all of which were solved by that Act.

Lieb, Charles. *Explaining the New Copyright Law: A Guide to Legitimate Photocopying of Copyrighted Materials*. New York: Assn. of American Publishers, 1977.

This pamphlet was written by the counsel to the AAP on copyright matters, as a short and simple guide to anyone who needs to know the key provisions of the Copyright Act of 1976 and the agreed ancillary guidelines for permissible photocopying for educational and interlibrary-lending uses.

History

Madison, Charles A. *Book Publishing in America*. New York: McGraw-Hill, 1966; reissue, R. R. Bowker, 1974.

A large book that covers its subject from colonial beginnings down to the year of publication. Though organized by historical periods, it recites the history of leading individual publishers and publishing houses in detail, and thus provides a mine of information, including a useful chronology of publishing events. Certain of the author's freely expressed opinions and evaluations are open to debate.

Tebbel, John. *A History of Book Publishing in the United States.* Vol. 1: *The Creation of an Industry, 1630–1865.* Vol. 2: *The Expansion of an Industry, 1865–1919.* New York: R. R. Bowker, 1972 (Vol. 1) & 1974 (Vol. 2). Vols. 3 & 4 in prep.

This is the definitive and most comprehensive work of its kind. It is scholarly, but written in an interesting and often entertaining style. Must reading for anyone who has a serious interest in book publishing. Volume 3, scheduled for publication in 1978, will cover the years 1919 to 1945; Volume 4, also in preparation, will cover 1945 to the present.

Management

Bohne, Harold, and von Ierssel, Harry. *Publishing: The Creative Business.* Toronto: University of Toronto Press, 1973.

A practical manual on the organization of the business management of a publishing enterprise. Specifics on financing, accounting, budgeting, and other service functions. The best work of its kind.

Nagger, Jean V., ed. *The Money Side of Publishing.* New York: Assn. of American Publishers, 1976.

Proceedings of a 1976 conference sponsored by the General Publishing Division of the AAP. There are reports on such topics as sources of capital, cash flow, working capital, analyzing operating statements and balance sheets, budgeting, and controlling costs. Simple and informative reading for nonfinancial people.

Mass Market Paperbacks

Petersen, Clarence. *The Bantam Story: Thirty Years of Paperback Publishing.* New York: Bantam, 1975.

A readable and reasonably objective statement of the history and publishing practices of the largest firm in its field and of the development of the American paperback industry in general.

Smith, Roger H. *Paperback Parnassus.* Boulder, Colo.: Westview, 1976.

A comprehensive report on the paperback industry, its publishing practices, its marketing methods, its economic condition, and its relations with authors and hardcover publishers. Rather dull reading but highly informative.

Scholarly Publishing

Hawes, Gene R. *To Advance Knowledge: A Handbook on American University Press Publishing.* New York: American University Press Services, 1967.

A systematic exposition of the objectives, policies, practices, and economics of scholarly book publishing in America, with emphasis on the history and then-current problems of university presses.

Nemeyer, Carol A. *Scholarly Reprint Publishing in the United States.* New York: R. R. Bowker, 1972.

A scholarly study of the structure, development and economics of facsimile reprint publishing of scholarly works—largely of documentary nature—that had been out of print for some years. A surge of such publishing came in the 1960s, when libraries had federal funds for the purchase of books of this kind.

Miscellaneous

Anderson, Charles B., ed. *Bookselling in America and the World.* New York: Quadrangle, 1975.

A symposium on the history of bookselling and of the American Booksellers Association, written by several authorities and published in celebration of the ABA's 75th anniversary. The editor is the "dean" of U.S. booksellers.

Book Publishing in the U.S.S.R. Cambridge: Harvard University Press, 1971.

A volume that contains the reports of two State Department-sponsored delegations of U.S. publishers who visited the U.S.S.R. in 1962 and 1970. The report of the second delegation builds upon that of the first; taken together they make informative reading for anyone who is interested in how book publishing is conducted under authoritarian control in a communist society.

Chappell, Warren. *A Short History of the Printed Word.* New York: Knopf, 1970.

A handsomely illustrated account of important people and events in the history of printing, written by a distinguished designer. Must reading for anyone who has a special interest in the design and production of books.

Colby, Jean Poindexter. *Writing, Illustrating, and Editing Children's Books.* New York: Hastings House, 1967.

A comprehensive guide to the unique methods and procedures of this specialized kind of book publishing. It emphasizes the importance of author-illustrator-editor relations in the production of successful titles for young readers.

Downs, Robert B. *Books that Changed America.* New York: Macmillan, 1970.

A very interesting and perceptive discussion of 25 books that have profoundly influenced our nation's culture and politics over two centuries of its history, ranging from Thomas Paine's *Common Sense* to Rachel Carson's *Silent Spring.*

Hackett, Alice Payne, and Burke, Henry James. *Eighty Years of Best Sellers, 1895–1975.* New York: R. R. Bowker, 1977.

An alluring reference work that lists the best-sellers of each year, together with notes on the social and historical setting for each listing.

Peters, Jean, ed. *The Bookman's Glossary*, 5th ed. New York: R. R. Bowker, 1975.

A reference book that defines and explains some 1,600 terms used in publishing, printing, bookselling, the antiquarian book trade, and the new technology of book production. Especially useful to editors.

Sutherland, James, ed. *The Oxford Book of Literary Anecdotes.* Oxford: Oxford University Press, 1975.

A highly entertaining collection of excerpts from the letters, notes, diaries, and other personal or published papers of both famous and obscure writers that cover some thirteen hundred years and almost every subject that one can think of. Excellent bedside reading matter.

PERIODICALS

The Bookseller. London: J. Whitaker, by subscription.

The British counterpart of Bowker's *Publishers Weekly*, edited with a broader international interest. Must reading for U.S. publishers who are engaged in book exporting or multinational publishing ventures.

Bookviews. New York: R. R. Bowker, by subscription.

An attractive new monthly edited for the general reader who has a special interest in books and authors and who feels that the regular review media do not provide sufficiently comprehensive coverage of the new books published each year. Each issue includes a large number of short reviews classified by subject matter.

Publishers Weekly. New York: R. R. Bowker, by subscription.

Covers news, views, trends, and personnel notes of U.S. book publishing and book trade; also provides advance notices of almost all the important books published each year, either by short reviews or by publishers' announcements. Must reading for anyone who is seriously interested in the book business.

Scholarly Publishing. Toronto: University of Toronto Press, by subscription.

A quarterly edited principally for readers who are at, or connected with, university presses. The articles usually are lively and timely, and are of interest and value to those commercial publishers who also publish many scholarly books.

Index